PUEBLO DECO

PUEBLO DECO

THE ART DECO
ARCHITECTURE
OF THE SOUTHWEST

Marcus Whiffen
and
Carla Breeze

Photographs by
Carla Breeze

UNIVERSITY OF NEW MEXICO PRESS
Albuquerque

Library of Congress Cataloging in Publication Data

Whiffen, Marcus.
  Pueblo deco.

  Includes bibliographical references and index.
   1. Decoration and ornament, Architectural—Southwest,
New.   2. Art deco—Southwest, New.   3. Architecture—
Southwest, New.   I. Breeze, Carla.   II. Title.
NA3508.6.W48   1983   720'.978   83-23467

Design by Emmy Ezzell

Printed in Japan
Text © 1984 by Marcus Whiffen.
Photographs © 1984 by Carla Breeze.
All rights reserved.
International Standard Book Number 0-8263-0676-4.
Library of Congress Catalog Card Number 83-23467.
First edition.

The publication of this book was made possible by a grant
from the National Endowment for the Arts.

Dedicated to the memory of
Bonnie Hontas

CONTENTS

CONTENTS

CONTENTS

ACKNOWLEDGMENT

The authors wish to thank the following: Bettye Abbiss, Orie Bachechi, Joe Boehning, Kathleen Brooker, Mary L. Carlander, Wayne Decker, Susan V. Dewitt, Robert Frankeberger, Ted Friese, Billy G. Garrett, Ray Graham of Ovenwest, David Gebhard, Sara Gresham, Charles Basset Hammond, Gordon Heck, Steve Hoagland, Byron Johnson, Diana Kordan, Carleen Lazell, Marie Loyd, Warren McArthur, Jr., Leslie Mahoney, Ron Mastick, Billy Merrell, Bryce Pearsall of Lescher and Mahoney, Warren Pendleton, Bill Rubidoux, Bill J. Shelton, Merle Shelton, W. O. Webster of Genesco, Louise Westlake.

PUEBLO DECO

PART ONE

INTRODUCTION

1

TWO
EXHIBITIONS

Adolf Loos would have been dismayed. It was seven years since he had written the famous pamphlet in which, with the aid of psychology, sociology, and economics, he had proved that the use of ornament, in the twentieth century, indicated criminality or degeneracy. Yet here was an exhibition whose buildings proclaimed that ornament was, as Ruskin had said, "the all in all of the thing to be done." Or if not quite the all in all—for picturesque effect was certainly a consideration too—something not far short of it. The irony of it was that this was not only in the America in which the Viennese architect had lived and which he greatly admired, but in the very region where an architecture that could not be faulted by the tenets of his ascetic and singularly unViennese philosophy already existed.

Whether Irving Gill, the creator of that architecture, had read *Ornament und Verbrechen* (Ornament and Crime) we do not know. According to Frank Lloyd Wright's eldest son, Lloyd, himself no enemy of ornament, Gill was an admirer of Loos's older compatriot, Otto Wagner; so it is likely enough that he had. We do know that until January 1911 most people interested in the matter assumed that Gill would be the architect of the exhibition so temerariously planned by the city of San Diego, California, which then had a population of less than 80,000, to join San Francisco in celebrating the opening of the Panama Canal. In the 1890s a style of architecture derived from the missions built by the Franciscans in the late eighteenth and early nineteenth centuries had swept California. Gill, who had arrived in San Diego from Chicago in 1893, took up this Mission style and proceeded to dehistoricize and rationalize it. In 1914 he was to design, in the Walter L. Dodge house in Los Angeles, a building that in photographs could easily be postdated by ten or twelve years and taken for an example of what is now generally called the International style. Had Irving Gill been the architect of the Panama California Exposition of 1915, America might have joined the modern movement that owed so much to Loos fifteen years before it did.

When the time came, an easterner, Bertram Grosvenor Goodhue, was appointed architect—largely on his own recommendation. Shortly before the turn of the century Goodhue, best known for his Gothic designs, traveled in Mexico with the millionaire Sylvester Baxter and the photographer Henry Peabody, studying Spanish Colonial architecture. The importance of this field trip for American architecture is comparable to that of the one made by McKim, Mead and White along the New England coast in search of colonial buildings in 1877. (The modes of progression differed, however, for McKim, Mead and White walked whereas Baxter, Goodhue, and Peabody rode in Baxter's private railroad car.) In 1901 appeared *Spanish-Colonial Architecture in Mexico,* with a text by Baxter, photographs by Peabody, and drawings by Goodhue. This book had much to do with the appointment of the last as architect of the San Diego exhibition, whose "atmosphere"—in 1915 the word when used metaphorically was still put between quotation marks—was to be that of "a Spanish City of flower-grown white surfaces, reflecting the sunlight and the history and romance of Southern California."[1]

The profuse ornament which set off those white surfaces varied in character. In the Foreign Arts Building it was sixteenth-century Plateresque; in most of the other buildings—including the California Building, in which Goodhue combined reworked details from several churches in Mexico he had studied fifteen years before—it was eighteenth-century Churrigueresque or Ultra-Baroque. Few of the visitors to the exhibition can have been aware of such distinctions. As the author of the article in the *Architectural Record* wrote, "the architectural style selected for the exposition at San Diego is one which is as generally unfamiliar in this country as it is historically and logically appropriate in its use here."[2] The marriage of what was seen as historical and logical appropriateness and unfamiliarity was a fruitful one, and Balboa Park became the birthplace of that Spanish Colonial revival which by 1925 had become a nationwide craze.[3]

That year, 1925, saw another exhibition whose architects, with a few important exceptions, ignored the theories of Adolf Loos—an exhibition which, being international, was to have an even greater influence than that in San Diego ten years before. But for the outbreak of World War I this exhibition, first planned in 1912 as the French answer to the German challenge in the field of design, would have been held in 1915. In 1925, as the Exposition des Arts Décoratifs et Industriels Modernes, it had as its stated purpose the showing of works of decorative and industrial art of new inspiration and true originality; the historical styles were "strictly prohibited." Germany was invited too late for effective participation and declined. Another absentee was the United States, Herbert Hoover as secretary of commerce writing that no modern design was being produced here.

The buildings in the Paris 1925 exhibition that find mention most often in histories of architecture are the theater, designed by Auguste Perret in his reductive-classical manner, the Expressionist greenhouse, attached to the Austrian pavilion, by the German Peter Behrens (who was given the commission as director of the School of Architecture in the University of Vienna), the Russian pavilion, of glass and wood, by Konstantin Melnikov, and Le Corbusier's Pavillon de l'Esprit Nouveau, a model dwelling unit named for the magazine through which he and Amedée Ozenfant had disseminated their doctrine of Purism. But what impressed most visitors to the exhibition were not these, nor the other foreign pavilions on the right bank of the Seine, but the French buildings on the main esplanade, which ran from the Pont Alexandre III to the Place des Invalides, with the dome of Les Invalides forming a focal feature on the horizon to the south.[4]

Conspicuous among these were the pavilions of the four great department stores: Les Grands Magasins du Louvre, Bon Marché, Les Galeries Lafayette, and Le Printemps. Then there were the Sèvres pavilion, dwarfed rather by eight Brobdingnagian vases, the pavilion of the booksellers G. Crès & Cie., and—most admired of all, for its contents as well as its architecture—the Hôtel du Collectionneur, in the form of a single-story house furnished with the work of the *ébéniste* Emile-Jacques Ruhlmann and his collaborators. Two of the regional pavilions, those of Nancy and Eastern France and of Lyons and St. Etienne, faced each other across the esplanade, while at its south end the glass fountain of René Lalique shone by night with "fairylike" effect.[5]

Tony Garnier, the architect of the Lyons and St. Etienne pavilion, is well known for his plan for an industrial city; Henri Sauvage, architect of the Printemps pavilion, finds mention in histories of modern architecture for a terraced apartment block in Paris—whose simplicity must have made the concrete and glass-domed extravaganza of the Pavillon Primavera, as the Printemps pavilion was called, a surprise indeed. But what of the architects of the other buildings mentioned in the last paragraph: A. Laprade, L. Boileau, J. Hiriart, G. Tribaut, G. Beau, P. Patout, A. Ventre, P. de Bourgeois? For them you will search the indexes of histories of modern architecture in vain.[6]

If any of those buildings had been a masterpiece there would be more cause for complaint than there is. None was. It was in what they had in common despite superficial differences that were often striking enough— their style, in short—that their importance lay. Historically, as critics recognized at the time, this style owed much to the Viennese Secession of the turn of the century. Philosophically, it expressed the proposition that architecture could be modern without being *outré,* and without abandoning ornament. Formally, it was marked by the strictest symmetry of plan, while exteriors, though composed of clean-cut, blocklike forms reminiscent of the Neoclassicism of the late eighteenth century, tended to follow Baroque principles, with the masses stepping up to a dominant center. Columns and pilasters, usually fluted or reeded, were much used, but rarely had anything that could be taken for a capital; they might support a frieze without any architrave (the Nancy and G. Crés & Cie. pavilions), sculptural groups (Galeries Lafayette pavilion) or planters (Pavillon Primavera), but never a complete entablature; cornices were eschewed altogether. The columns of the G. Crés & Cie. pavilion were attached to spur walls like Old Kingdom Egyptian columns; the frieze above them was ornamented with a running chevron or zigzag, a motif rarely employed in the exhibition, although it was to be the leitmotif of many designs in the style named after it. A sunburst, another favorite device with American architects of the Art Deco, filled the upper part of the entrance aedicule of the Galeries Lafayette pavilion. When panels of sculpture were employed, as in the Hôtel du Collectionneur and the pavilions of Nancy and Eastern France, they were in the lowest relief.

Paris 1925 would have been a different exhibition and might have had a very different impact in America if Germany, the Germany of the Deutscher Werkbund and the Bauhaus, had been represented. The absence of the

United States as a participant mattered little; thousands of Americans, including 108 official delegates from government bodies and societies concerned with design, visited the exhibition, and the architects among them read the message in their French confreres' buildings. With the Spanish Colonial revival at its height and therefore likely soon to pall, the message came at the right moment; America needed a new ornamental style, and here was one that was not only new but modern into the bargain. And so was born the architectural style of the later 1920s and early 1930s that used to be called Modernistic but is now by common consent called Art Deco. Since Modernistic had derogatory overtones, the change is to be welcomed. The term *Art Deco* is appropriate in that it was the Exposition des Arts Décoratifs et Industriels Modernes that supplied exemplars and inspiration. But American Art Deco was not simply a European import. It owed much of its character to circumstances that were peculiar to America.

2

AMERICAN ART DECO

The most important of the circumstances peculiar to America that formed the character of American Art Deco was the existence of the skyscraper. In 1925 there were no skyscrapers in Europe; in America, the skyscraper, as a multistory, metal-frame building, had a history that went back forty years. The problem of how to give unity to buildings of more than five or six stories had been solved by Louis Sullivan (not without broad hints from certain loft buildings of the mid-nineteenth century in Philadelphia), and Sullivan had also evolved a style of ornament for its decoration. It may be that connections are to be traced between Sullivan's ornament, and that of his longtime assistant George Grant Elmslie, and Art Deco. Yet on analysis Art Deco ornament proves to be as different from Sullivan's as the latter was from the contemporary Art Nouveau of Europe.[7] It seems reasonable to accept the account of the matter given by the prominent Art Deco architect, Ely Jacques Kahn, who granted that Sullivan's ornament was "in its exuberance . . . astounding," when he wrote: "At his death (in 1924) Sullivan's influence stopped, largely because of the purely personal quality of his work and more particularly because the involved detail he produced became somewhat tiresome."[8] A decade that worshipped speed had no time for the intricacies of the Sullivanesque.

By the second decade of the twentieth century the ever-increasing height of the skyscraper was leading to ever-increasing congestion in the business quarters of American cities. To remedy this, legislation was sought, and in 1916 New York passed the first zoning act. The model for ordinances eventually adopted by all major American cities, this act divided the city into zones according to use and limited the height of walls next to the street according to the zone and the width of the street, requiring that the building above that be set back behind an imaginary line drawn from the center of the street through the top of the street wall; upon one quarter of its lot a building could rise to any height. Thus the overall form of the typical skyscraper of the 1920s, with its setbacks at different levels, was determined by law.

The next major event in skyscraper history was a competition. In 1922 Colonel Robert McCormick, owner of the *Chicago Tribune,* resolved that "the world's greatest newspaper" should be housed in "the world's most beautiful office building." Two hundred and sixty-three designs were received from twenty-three countries. The first premium went to John M. Howells and Raymond M. Hood, and theirs is the Gothic-belfried Tribune Tower that stands today. It was the design of the runner-up, the Finnish architect Eliel Saarinen, that came as a revelation to many architects, while Sullivan himself wrote an article praising it. Not only did Saarinen fit his design into the "zoning envelope" allowed by the city ordinances with perfect efficiency and unrivalled suavity, he clothed it with detail that was Gothic in origin and feeling but, as Henry Russell Hitchcock has said, "stylized nearly to the point of absolute originality."[9] In the elevations he followed Sullivan's system of uninterrupted verticals while omitting the cornices beneath which Sullivan had stopped his—in this, too, setting a precedent for the Art Deco skyscrapers to come.

When the *Tribune* competition was held, there already stood in Chicago, little noticed, a precursor of Art Deco that should not be passed over. This was the Franklin Building, a twelve-story printing works for a firm that specialized in color printing. The architect was George Nimmons, a leading industrial and commercial architect whose buildings usually show Gothic detail. In this case he had an unusual client, who was described by the *Architectural Record* in 1915 as "one of the insurgents of the laity who has turned entirely against all that is conventional and particularly classical in architectural design" and who "required that his building be designed entirely with straight lines, as he had a prejudice against the curve, that there be no conventional architecture whatever in its design, that it have a brilliant color introduced through the medium of tile or terra cotta, and that the art of printing should be indicated in its decoration."[10] With paintings reproduced in colored tile over the entrance and on the first-story spandrels, and abstract patterns in colored tile and terra-cotta on the other spandrels and on the gable wall of the studio at the top of the facade, the Franklin Building was as prophetic of Art Deco as Gill's Dodge House was of the International style.

But New York, not Chicago, was to be the Art Deco city par excellence; its architects were more open to European influence, and the new style coincided with an unprecented boom in office building. The Barclay-Vesey Building, by McKenzie, Voorhees and Gmelin, was the first Art Deco skyscraper—Art Deco "avant la lettre," for it was begun in 1923. The general plainness of the exterior, which owes much to Saarinen's *Tribune* design, is relieved by discreetly placed low reliefs of vegetation and animals and human figures, and in the lobby there is more of the same—so much more that Lewis Mumford was led to write that it was "as gaily . . . decorated as a village street in a strawberry festival"—in metal. The chevron or zigzag, to be used so much in Art Deco that one of the names given to the style has been Zigzag Moderne, is absent from the Barclay-Vesey Building; it made its first appearance in New York on the Insurance Center Building of 1926–27, by Buchman and Kahn. Ely Jacques Kahn, whose views on Sullivan have been quoted, was perhaps the most inventive of the architects of the American Art Deco, as well as the most prolific. Of catholic taste, at the Paris exhibition he had been most struck by Joseph Hoffmann's Austrian Pavilion and Peter Behrens's greenhouse adjoining it, and elements from the Secessionist and Expressionist styles they represented were to meet in his work.

Kahn was the leading exponent of the use of color in architecture, beginning with the Park Avenue Building of 1927, with its spandrels and striping of red, blue, and yellow glazed terra-cotta. Another architect with a strong interest in color was Raymond Hood; his News Building (1929–30) has spandrels of red and black brick to set off the white brick cladding of the piers, while the blue-green terra-cotta facing of the spandrels of the McGraw-Hill Building (1930–31) is shaded from dark below to lighter above to give an effect of sunlight even on an overcast day.

This is not the place for a detailed account of New York Art Deco, which has received exemplary treatment elsewhere.[11] Yet mention must be made of Joseph Urban, who as manager of the New York branch of the Wiener Werkstatte, opened in 1919, was instrumental in familiarizing Americans with the products of the Viennese Secessionist tradition and thus preparing the way for Art Deco. Urban's best-known building was the Ziegfeld Theater of 1926–27. Never committed to unrelieved verticality, as many Art Deco architects were, in his New School for Social Research of 1929–30 he was one of the first to employ the effects, inspired by the work of the German Expressionist Erich Mendelsohn, that were soon to give American architecture a new style in the Streamline Moderne.

The earliest Art Deco skyscraper outside New York was the twenty-six-story Telephone Building in San Francisco. It was completed in 1925 and so, as with that other monument to Alexander Graham Bell, the Barclay-Vesey Building, there can be no question of any influence from Paris; the architects were James Miller and Timothy Pflueger. In an article in *Architecture* in 1926, J. S. Cahill tells us that the early studies revealed "hints of Gothic influence."[12] "But these faded out completely as the design neared maturity, and, of all the definite historical styles extant, this building shows a frankly expressed trace of only one, and that, strange to say, is Chinese!" (Not so very strange, surely, in view of San Francisco's trade links with the Orient and the large Chinese population of the city.)

The San Francisco Telephone Building was, to quote Cahill again, "a complete surprise to the architectural profession and a positive delight to the public at large." (Of how many prominent buildings of this size in recent history could it be said that they delighted the public?) Miller and Pflueger became the most successful Art Deco architects in San Francisco, as well as the best. Their masterpiece is 450 Sutter Street, with bay windows and ornament of Mayan inspiration on the spandrels and in the lobby, which was completed in 1930, while the astonishing front of the Paramount Theater across the bay at Oakland, completed in 1932, challenges Urban's Ziegfield Theater for the prize for originality in this field of design.

Most of the larger American cities acquired Art Deco skyscrapers in the late twenties; one thinks of the Guardian Building in Detroit (Smith, Hinchman and Grills, 1929), the Northern Life Tower in Seattle (Joseph W. Wilson, 1929), and the Richfield Building in Los Angeles. The last, which was completed in 1929 to the design of Morgan, Walls, and Clements with an exterior of black brick with details picked out in gold—a mode started by Hood's American Radiator Building in New York (1924)—is no more. Yet in Los Angeles, better than anywhere outside New York, one can still see the impact of Art Deco on a wide range of building types—though film stars, regrettably, preferred Spanish or Tudor for their homes. Among apartment buildings, Leland Bryant's Sunset Towers (1927) still dominates a stretch of the boulevard from which it takes its name. For a small but striking example of the black-and-gold mode there is the Crocker Bank (originally the Selig Building) on Western Avenue, designed by Arthur Harvey in 1931, which is pure Art Deco in its ornament though in its curved corner of glass bricks it hints at the Streamline Moderne to come. Then there are the theaters of Gilbert S. Underwood and F. Charles Lee (whose Fox Theater in Phoenix was destroyed in 1974). And one of the masterpieces of Art Deco anywhere is Bullock's Wilshire Store. Designed by John and Donald Parkinson and Jack Peters and completed in 1929, Bullock's Wilshire, with its fine materials and finishes and precision of detail and the sense of opulence they convey, stands out among its neighbors like a Rolls Royce among Fords and Chevrolets.

The tower of Bullock's Wilshire is somewhat reminiscent of that of Eliel Saarinen's railroad terminal in Helsinki (1910–14). Saarinen's near success in the *Tribune* competition would naturally have aroused interest in his earlier works, so that in this case it may be safe to talk of influence. The same building may have been the original source of that favorite Art Deco form, the scalloped arch—which is not to say that every architect who used it was consciously imitating Saarinen, for such things quickly become part of the common vocabulary of a style. In looking for the sources of American Art Deco it is necessary to distinguish between designs that may have served as models and those that prefigured the style without influencing it directly. To be numbered among the latter, surely, is the interior of the Sommerfeld House in Berlin, with its zigzags and triangles and stepped stair-parapet, which was designed in 1921 by none other than Walter Gropius. On the other hand, the Expressionism of Hamburg and that of the Amsterdam School, with their rich textural and sculptural effects in brick, must have been directly influential, for examples of both were published in America in the early twenties and one may be sure that they were not overlooked by traveling architects. Among cisatlantic influences there was the work of Frank Lloyd Wright between 1915 and 1924 in which he used patterned concrete blocks—"textile blocks" as he called them. The patterns were abstractions of Mayan ornament, which was incorporated in a less abstract form into the Art Deco repertory by Miller and Pflueger, as we have noted, and by the architect of the Kress stores, Edward Sibbert, among others.[13] In 1925 the English architect Alfred Bossom went so far as to suggest in the *American Architect* that "a great American national style" could be built upon Mayan architecture "as a foundation," for it was "a very small step from the Tikal pyramid at [*sic*] Guatemala to a zoning law building of Broadway"; he illustrated his article with a perspective of a thirty-five-story building "designed after primitive American [i.e., Mayan] motives."[14]

3

ART DECO'S PLACE
IN HISTORY

Few American towns are without examples of Modernistic architecture. During the ascendancy of the International Style they seemed to represent what was worst in the immediate past. Today they are not so much disliked as simply disregarded. Tomorrow they will doubtless be found to have period charm. Some of them—though perhaps not very many—must have more than that. [15]

So wrote one of the authors of this book fifteen years ago. The tomorrow referred to was not long in coming. In the year in which those words appeared in print, 1969, the first considered reassessment of American Art Deco and its successor the Streamline Moderne was published, by David Gebhard. [16] By 1972 the study of Art Deco had achieved academic respectability, as the proceedings of the joint annual meeting of the College Art Association and the Society of Architectural Historians, held that year in San Francisco, demonstrated. In 1980 the style received what many will consider a more significant kind of recognition when James Stirling, in his address on being presented with the Royal Gold Medal of the Royal Institute of British Architects, named the Art Deco of New York among the things by which he had been influenced in his work. [17]

If period charm, or period character, is what attracts many people to Art Deco, that is a measure of the success of its architects. Optimists rather than idealists, they were intent on creating works of architecture that should be, first of all, contemporary—expressive of their time, of their present. It is in this that Art Deco differs most profoundly from the International style, for the architecture of the International style was an expression of an ideal, or a set of ideals, rather than of any present actuality. An International-style building can never have period charm because it always belonged to the future, an ideal future which never came although its image still has the power to move.

The International style and Art Deco coexisted in the international scene for little more than ten years—in America, where the International style did not establish itself until the thirties and Streamline Moderne began to overtake Art Deco early in the same decade, for barely half as long. As Gebhard pointed out, these three styles were all machine-age styles in their different ways—the International because it expressed the machine symbolically in the precision of its forms and finishes, Art Deco because its ornament was "purposefully repetitive and . . . conveyed the feeling that if it were not produced by machine it should have been," Streamline because of its borrowings of forms from modern transportation machines, ocean liners, trains, and cars. It was the obvious modernity of Streamline Moderne that made it immediately acceptable to the public (and to critics who had been uncomfortable with Art Deco, which sometimes could only be regarded as modern because it was not anything else), while for architects and their clients it had what in the thirties was the great advantage of cheapness, since it required neither the costly materials so much used in Art Deco nor, unless horizontal trim in cement or metal is to be reckoned as ornament, any ornament at all.

As a style of architecture that was also, and primarily, a style of ornament, Art Deco invites comparison with Rococo and Art Nouveau. It would be an ardent Decophile indeed who claimed that it fared well in either comparison. Art Deco is not, perhaps, one of the great styles of history; no really great architect took it up; the depression came before it could reach its highest development; its masterpieces are only masterpieces of Art Deco. Yet it was a style that gave scope to the kind of creativity that even minor talents may possess.

4

ART DECO
IN THE SOUTHWEST

By dictionary definition, the American Southwest comprises the six southerly states that stretch from the west bank of the Mississippi to the borders of California and Nevada: Louisiana, Arkansas, Oklahoma, Texas, New Mexico, and Arizona. Here we are not concerned with the first three of those states, nor with east Texas. Our Southwest is approximately the western half of the dictionary's Southwest. It is a region, which, in conjunction with southern Colorado, has a history, and an architectural history, that differ in important respects from those of the rest of the United States. In prehistoric times it was inhabited by Indians who lived in towns, or pueblos, which were built of stone and mass adobe—the only Indians on the continent north of Mexico to live in permanent settlements built of those materials. In their most distinctive form these pueblos consisted of large terraced apartment houses, such as may still be seen in the pueblo of San Geronimo de Taos today. The first Europeans to arrive in the region were the Spaniards, who had their own adobe-building tradition. They introduced the making of adobe bricks, and a technique of construction was established that with minor modifications—for instance, modern adobes (as the bricks are called) are an inch or two smaller in each dimension than colonial adobes—has been employed ever since. Architecturally, the most remarkable products of the Spanish occupation were the churches, in which European forms were adapted to construction in adobe by Indian labor.

CHAPTER FOUR

Characterized by broad, unbroken surfaces and massive, sculptural effects, they were unlike any other churches in the Spanish dominions or in Spain itself.

Extreme conservatism, due in large part to the limitations of adobe, marked the colonial architecture of the Southwest. The first architectural product of the American occupation was the so-called Territorial style, in which wooden trim of a simple Greek Revival character was added to buildings whose long, low lines and flat roofs continued the Spanish tradition. Most of the styles current in the East in the second half of the nineteenth century followed, to be joined in the first years of the twentieth century by one from the West, the Californian Mission style. Then, in 1905, a revival of the forms of early pueblo architecture, both Indian and Spanish, was initiated on the campus of the University of New Mexico by its third president, George W. Tight. Practicality, as well as historical sentiment, made this Pueblo style popular for buildings of many types. Soon New Mexico had what was very rare if not unique in the United States, a regional style that permeated architecture at every level, while in Arizona, if not in Texas, the Pueblo style was much favored for domestic work.

The Spanish Colonial revival of southern California provenance never got much of a showing in New Mexico, owing to the popularity of the Pueblo style. In Arizona the case was different, and there are major works in the style by, most notably, Roy Place of Tucson and Leslie Mahoney of Phoenix. In turning from Spanish to Art Deco, as they both did, Place and Mahoney followed a course chosen by architects of their generation all over the United States. Unique to the Southwest, on the other hand, was the process of regionalization that Art Deco underwent there, resulting in a variant of the style that may be called Pueblo Deco.

The Fred Harvey Company did much to pave the way for this development in the first quarter of the century. Recognizing the potential of an architectural expression of the southwestern experience for attracting tourists, they revived the Spanish and Indian styles in their hotels. The Alvarado Hotel of 1902 in Albuquerque was their first large-scale success. Designed in the Mission style by Charles Whittlesey, this had an Indian Room decorated by Mary Jane Coulter, utilizing Indian motifs to enhance the merchandizing of Indian arts. It is not too much to say that this venture created the general interest in Indian artifacts and architecture. Later Coulter designed El Tovar, at the Grand Canyon, inspired by the Hopi, and El Navajo Hotel in Gallup, which with its Navajo-inspired decorations was probably the most influential of these hotels.[18] It was the Harvey houses, more than any other single factor, that instilled in architects and designers an enthusiasm for decoration derived from the Pueblo and Navajo cultures.

In some Pueblo Deco designs, such as the KiMo Theater in Albuquerque and the Southern Pacific Station at Casa Grande, Pueblo-style forms and massing are combined with ornament from North American Indian sources; in others, such as the Maisel Building in Albuquerque, Indian motifs are used in a frankly modern architectural setting. These motifs were never part of any North American Indian architecture, but were taken from pottery, basket work, jewelry, and textiles; their use in architecture represents a creative translation of forms from one medium into another and so cannot be characterized as revivalism. (Here a comparison suggests itself between the KiMo Theater and its exact contemporary in Los Angeles, the Mayan Theater of Morgan, Walls and Clements, in which the exclusive use of Mayan *architectural* motifs can only be seen as revivalism—Pop revivalism, perhaps?) The angularity, repetitiveness, and abstraction of these Indian motifs were qualities they shared with much Art Deco ornament, so that aesthetic as well as regional considerations sanctioned their use.

What follows is not a history of Art Deco architecture in the Southwest, as the reader will perceive from the arrangement of the material, state by state, city by city, and building by building. It is, rather, a guide—but not a complete guide, for we have been selective. It may be that buildings have been omitted that would have been included had we been aware of them; certainly many buildings of which we were aware have been omitted because we judged them less deserving of inclusion than those which are included. In the process of selection our criteria were aesthetic. As a result, we believe, there is not a building illustrated in the following pages that is not worthy of preservation. If the reader comes to share our belief, and our respect for the often obscure and sometimes unknown architects who designed those buildings, this book will have served its purpose.

PART TWO

EXAMPLES

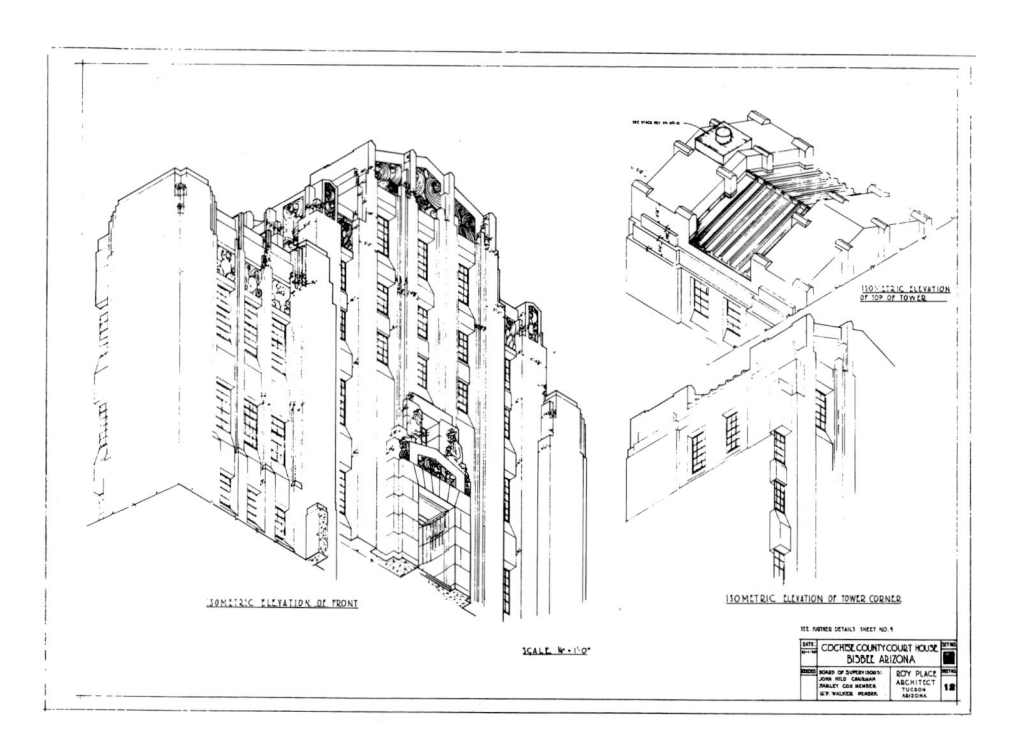

Cochise County Courthouse, Bisbee, Arizona, isometric of facade and tower details. (Arizona Architectural Archive, University of Arizona.)

ARIZONA

BISBEE

The **Cochise County Courthouse** was built in 1931, its dedication by Governor Hunt in August that year forming part of the celebrations of the fiftieth anniversary of the founding of the copper-mining town of Bisbee. Of concrete, with copper used for all piping and bronze for doors and stairwells, it cost $300,000. The architect was Roy Place of Tucson.

In 1928, Place, whose architectural career began twenty years before in the office of Shepley, Rutan and Coolidge in Boston, had built the Pima County Courthouse in Tucson in a self-confident Spanish-Colonial Baroque. For the building in Bisbee he turned for inspiration, as did other architects of courthouses in the early thirties, to the recent skyscrapers of New York, models that seemed appropriate enough at a time when courthouses, as Hitchcock and Seale have pointed out, "were becoming more and more public office buildings rather than public monuments."[19] But if the Cochise County Courthouse may be described as a miniature skyscraper it should certainly not be with any derogatory intent, for it is a work of architecture of real quality.

It stands in isolation, away from other buildings, at the foot of a steep hill of no particular character. In front is a balustraded terrace, reached by steps at the sides only—vehicular access is provided at the rear of the

See color plates, p. 75.

23

building—with two broad flights of steps leading up to the main entrance; terrace, steps, and facade are united in a self-contained, three-dimensional composition. The sense of self-containment is increased by the stepping-up of the facade from the three-bay, three-story wings, through the one-bay, four-story intermediate sections, to the three-bay, five-story center, through all of which the close-set piers rise uninterrupted to the parapets. Over the entrance, which is of stone, are two figures of miners which were modeled and cast from designs by the architect's son (and successor in practice) Lew Place, who was seventeen at the time. Ornament of a more abstract nature, consisting for the most part of fluted scrolls and cactus-like forms, is distributed on the upper part of the facade and above the windows along the sides of the building; of a more sculptural plasticity than most Art Deco ornament, it seems to owe something to its designer's exercise in the Churrigueresque three years earlier.

CASA GRANDE

See p. 76. The **Southern Pacific Station** at Casa Grande replaced a building destroyed by fire in June 1937. After the fire, the railroad's division superintendent in Tucson stated, according to the *Casa Grande Dispatch:* "We had plans ten years ago for a new station at Casa Grande, but the depression made it necessary to abandon the project." However, the railroad seemed to be in no hurry to rebuild, and it was not until March 31, 1939, that the paper was able to inform its readers that the president of the Southern Pacific had promised, in reply to a telegram from the vice-president of the Casa Grande Chamber of Commerce, that an early start would be made on the new station. From then on, things moved quickly. On April 21 the *Dispatch* reproduced a perspective and a plan of the projected building, which was described as being "of Pueblo design with Indian type of ornamental enrichments" while its construction was to be "semi-fireproof with wire fabric and stucco on the exterior and plaster and cement stucco on the interior." Bids for the contract, which required the work to be started on August 1 and completed in ninety days, were opened on July 21. The building was dedicated, in the presence of a large crowd of local people and a group of important Southern Pacific officials, on January 15, 1940.

Casa Grande Station was designed at the Southern Pacific headquarters in San Francisco, where the chief architect at the time was J. H. Christie;

25

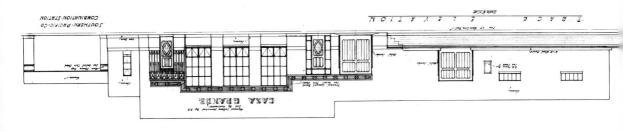

Southern Pacific Station, Casa Grande, Arizona, elevation. (Southern Pacific
Transportation Company.)

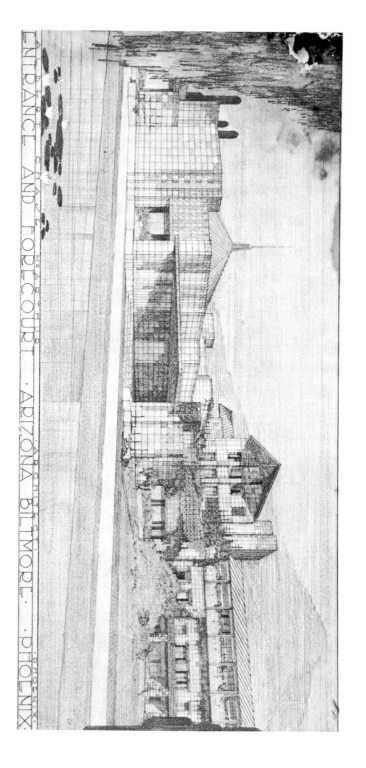

Arizona Biltmore Hotel, Phoenix, Arizona, perspective before design was finalized. (Warren McArthur, Jr.)

the drawings were signed by the staff architect William F. Meaney. It has three distinct parts. The central, and highest, contains the office, waiting room, and baggage room. To the north is the long freight room, and to the south a square porch (labeled "open waiting room" on the published plan) with four stout, primitivistic columns. Ornament, of Navajo rather than Hopi inspiration, is confined to the two main elevations of the central section, which are identical in design. Most of it is concentrated around the passenger entrances. These are flanked by grooved piers set back at windowsill level and ornamented with stepped pyramids; between the tops of the piers are diamonds within stepped diamonds, and the lintels are ornamented with bands of diamonds, arrows, and truncated pyramids, painted gold, yellow, and turquoise.[20] The baggage-room doorways are unembellished; they and the windows and the passenger entrances are tied together by a grooved band (of precast stucco sections) punctuated with diamonds in stepped diamonds and terminated at each end with a single fret.

Passenger trains no longer stop at Casa Grande and the station has not escaped indignity. One can only hope that a use will continue to be found for it. It merits preservation both as a building of intrinsic architectural quality and as the only example in Arizona (apparently) of the combination of Pueblo form and Indian ornament.

PHOENIX

When it was published in the *Architectural Record* on its completion in 1929, the **Arizona Biltmore Hotel** was described as being situated "some eight miles northeast of Phoenix." Its construction was the realization of a plan to give Phoenix a major resort hotel that had been conceived some years before by two brothers, Charles H. McArthur and Warren McArthur, Jr., who had come to Phoenix from Chicago in 1914. A third brother, Albert Chase McArthur, was the architect.

See pp. 77, 78, 79.

The father of the three, Warren McArthur, Sr., was one of Frank Lloyd Wright's first clients, and Albert, after a period at the Armour Institute of Technology and four years at Harvard, became an apprentice of Wright in The Studio in Oak Park, where he worked for two and a half years.[21] European travel followed; then in 1912 he returned to Chicago to practice, with an office in Sullivan's Schiller Building, in partnership with Arthur S.

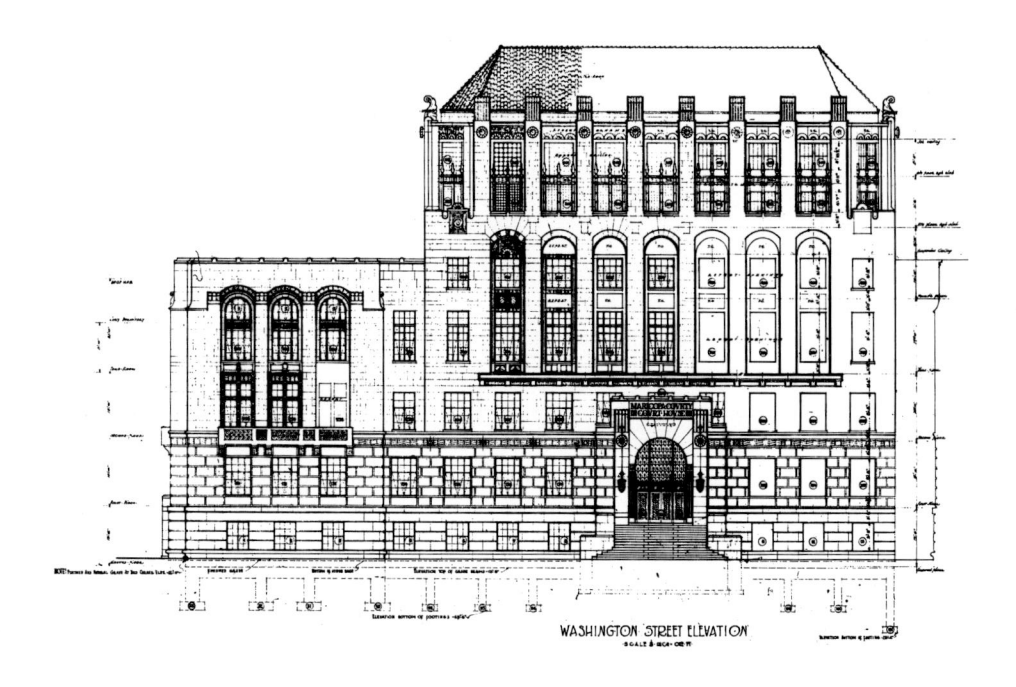

WASHINGTON STREET ELEVATION

City-County Building, Phoenix, Arizona, north elevation of Maricopa County section. (Facilities Management, Maricopa County.)

Facing page: First Interstate Bank (Title and Trust) Building, Phoenix, Arizona, east elevation. (Lescher and Mahoney.)

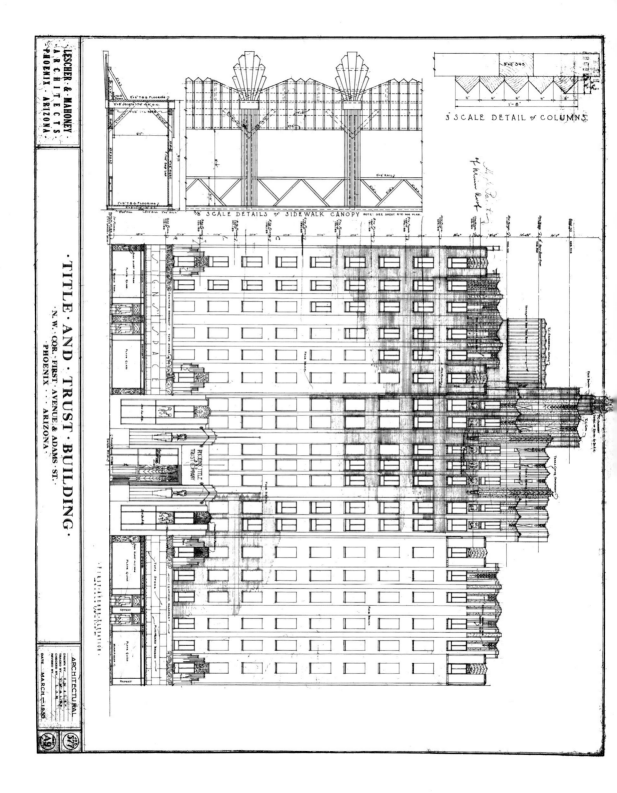

· LESCHER · & · MAHONEY ·
· A R C H I T E C T S ·
· PHOENIX · ARIZONA ·

· TITLE · AND · TRUST · BUILDING ·

· N. W. · COR · FIRST · AVENUE · & · ADAMS · ST ·
· PHOENIX · · · ARIZONA ·

3″ SCALE DETAIL of COLUMNS

3/8″ SCALE DETAILS of SIDEWALK CANOPY

· FIRST · AVENUE · ELEVATION ·

ARCHITECTURAL

DATE MARCH — 1930

A-9   577

Coffin. He moved to Arizona in 1925 and designed several houses in and around Phoenix before making the first designs for the Biltmore in 1927.

The Arizona Biltmore is sometimes attributed to Frank Lloyd Wright. Although it is true that Wright was involved, he was not the architect. Late in 1927 McArthur decided to use textile block slab construction, such as Wright had used in his houses of the early twenties in California, for the hotel and, thinking that Wright owned patents in it, asked his former master for permission. In a telegraphed reply, Wright endorsed the idea of using the technique and suggested that he should come to Phoenix to help McArthur start. In the event, Wright spent about four months in Phoenix beginning in January 1928 and received $10,000 for a license to use patents (which, it later transpired, he did not own) in the textile block slab construction. His employment on the project was brief, lasting some six or seven weeks before it was terminated by the client in response to complaints by the contractor and the project manager that his continual intervention was causing confusion on the job.[22]

In one sense the design of the Arizona Biltmore owes much to Wright. As the *Architectural Record* (probably quoting McArthur) put it, "the effort of the architect has been to design in the spirit of Frank Lloyd Wright's concepts of harmonizing the building with the terrain, of bringing out the inherent natural qualities of the materials used in the construction, and of considering as integral parts of the architectural scheme such elements as the furniture, the interior decoration, the system of illumination, and the like." And McArthur doubtless incorporated some of Wright's specific suggestions, though when Wright saw the hotel shortly before it was completed he remarked that he had thrown away the most important of them and that the building was "even worse than he thought it would be." McArthur's independence showed itself, to take a basic example, in the design of the concrete blocks. In his houses in California Wright had used square blocks, and in his telegram to McArthur he urged him to "make plans and elevations sixteen inch unit in all directions." In the Arizona Biltmore McArthur used blocks measuring eighteen inches long and thirteen and a half inches high, with a nine-foot (six-block) module to control the spacing of windows and other features.[23] Then the ornament on the blocks, the models for which were made to his design by the sculptor Emry Kopta, is very different from the ornament, always rectilinear and usually rectangular, on Wright's. Described by him as consisting of straight lines which are really subtle curves, it was a product of the study of light that was one of McArthur's special interests, being developed from an interference pattern.[24] Though hardly to be compared with Wright's Imperial Hotel in Tokyo, which McArthur admired greatly and by which he was clearly influenced, the Arizona Biltmore is a building of some originality which ranks high as an example of both hotel architecture and Art Deco.[25]

The **City-County Building,** to the west of Patriots Square in downtown Phoenix, was built in 1928 to house the Phoenix city courts and the courts and offices of Maricopa County. It cost the then very considerable sum of $1.2 million. The architect of the Maricopa County part of the building was Edward Neild of Shreveport, Louisiana; the architects for the city section, to the west, were Lescher and Mahoney; in the exterior elevations they were required to follow Neild's design. The bulk and scale and permanence of the materials and finishes of the City-County Building command respect, and Leslie Mahoney's Phoenixes flanking the west entrance are spirited members of their species. Yet it is a difficult building to like. The massive rustication of the first two stories, while not inappropriate in a public building, does not consort well with the Art Deco ornament—zigzags and botanical motifs—of the upper ones, and the overall effect, despite the richness of that ornament, is ponderous and even forbidding.

See pp. 80, 81.

The **First Interstate Bank Building** (until recently the Title and Trust Building) stands on the northwest corner of West Adams Street and First Avenue, with the principal entrance, above which the front is recessed to form a deep lightwell, on the latter. Built in April–December 1931, it is of ten stories (or thirteen counting the two-story penthouse and machine room above it), with a reinforced concrete frame, brick walls, and terra-cotta and tufa trim. The architects were Lescher and Mahoney. This partnership, which dominated the architectural scene in Phoenix for more than thirty years, was formed in 1922; Royal W. Lescher was the businessman, Leslie J. Mahoney the designer. Mahoney, who was born in Missouri in 1892, received his training as an architect in Los Angeles offices and in an atelier there sponsored by the Society of Beaux-Arts Architects in New York, to which a number of prominent Californian architects contributed their services. An admirer of Goodhue, his preference was for Spanish; an example of his Plateresque, the Palace West Theater, built in 1928 as the Orpheum, stands on Adams Street a block to the west of the First Interstate Bank Building.

See pp. 82, 83.

The ground story of the First Interstate Bank Building has been drastically altered. Originally there were four stores, with elaborate doors, on each front. Plate glass, sandblasted with a foliated pattern similar to that on the band of ornament (of tufa) under the second-floor windows, flanked these doors and also covered the pier at the corner of the building; large lights hung from the piers on either side of the First Avenue bank entrance and the main doors had metal grilles with carved glass above. All this went in the "modernization," though the marquee over the Adams Street entrace was spared. The upper stories are unchanged. The brickwork shows a refinement typical of the period, with the bricks, which were specially made in California, growing progressively lighter in color from bottom to top. But the glory of the building is its elevator lobby, which is twelve feet wide, seventy-seven feet long, and sixteen feet high. The walls are faced to their full height with verd antique, which is also used, in conjunction with travertine, on the floor. (Five different marbles are used inside the building.) The ornament on the three pairs of elevator doors, which in common with the directory at the foot of the stairs are of Monel metal, an alloy of nickel and copper, carries on the theme of that on the exterior of the building; the panels of foliage, in particular, are full of vitality. The architect wished to integrate the ceiling into the decorative scheme but the clients rejected his proposal and it is white and plain.[26] Nonetheless, for restrained richness this hall can have few equals in commercial architecture west of the Mississippi.

See p. 83.

The **Kress Store,** on the north side of Patriots Square, unlike its freestanding Art Deco neighbors, Luhrs Tower and the City-County Building, is street architecture, with only one exposed elevation. It was built in 1933, the architect being Edward Sibbert. A graduate of the Cornell School of Architecture, Sibbert was for a quarter of a century, from 1929 to 1954, responsible for the design of Kress stores throughout the country, as vicepresident of S. H. Kress & Co. Buildings. His New York store for the firm on Fifth Avenue, built in 1935, has Mayan-style reliefs on its front; notable for technical innovations, including artificial lighting of six times the intensity then usual in department stores, it won its architect a gold medal at the Pan American Exposition of 1940.

The terra-cotta-clad facade of the Kress Store is divided vertically into two parts, with the ground story, which is pierced above the marquee with windows which help to light the high sales hall, forming a basement for the upper part. In the latter there are eighteen windows to the office and warehouse floors. Grouped in threes within deep reveals, each group framed by a raised molding, these windows diminish upwards, those of the third floor being narrower than those of the second and those of the

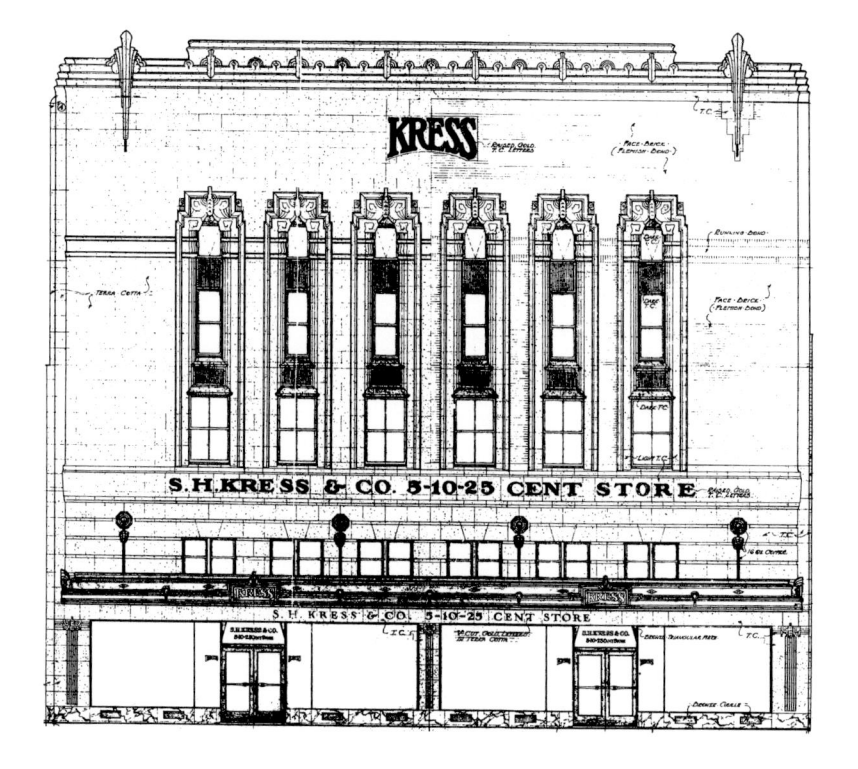

Kress Store, Phoenix, Arizona, south elevation. (Robert D. Frankeberger.)

Luhrs Tower, Phoenix, Arizona, preliminary design I.
(Arizona Collections, University Library, Arizona State
University.)

fourth being only half as high as those of the third—a treatment which results in an ambiguity of scale that tends to increase the apparent height of the building. The facade is crowned by a cornice consisting of five cavetto moldings, with a second cornice, consisting of two cavettos, rising above and behind the central section, over the windows. The upper cornice is connected to the lower by six curved, tubular brackets, colored green; halfway between it and the ends of the facade are elongated cartouches (for want of a better term) which from a distance look like nothing so much as huge lizards clinging to the top of the wall, although in fact they are composed entirely of abstract forms. (Similarly, the spiral ornaments above the fourth-floor windows may be seen as abstract forms or as flowers.) The description may still be written in the present tense, although by the time it appears in print the Kress Store will almost certainly have been demolished. In it Phoenix will lose not only an Art Deco building of distinction but one of its few examples of distinguished street architecture in any style.

Luhrs Tower, which stands to the south of Patriots Square, was built in 1929–30, the architects being Trost and Trost of El Paso, a firm that had been founded in 1903 and was for a quarter of a century the busiest firm of architects in the region. Henry Charles Trost, the eldest of three brothers, was the chief designer.[27] Born in Toledo, Ohio, he had practiced briefly in Pueblo, Colorado, and for about ten years in Chicago, where *inter alia* he designed for, and subsequently became president of, the Chicago Ornamental Iron Company. He moved to the Southwest—Tucson first—in 1898. Nothing if not versatile, he worked in many styles—Beaux-Arts Classical, Greek, Sullivanesque, Prairie, Mission, Pueblo, even Gothic on one occasion; his two buildings for the Owls Club in Tucson are in a mixture of Sullivanesque and Mission, the four built to his design for the Texas School of Mines and Metallurgy (now the University of Texas at El Paso) are of Bhutanese inspiration, while the Hotel Franciscan in Albuquerque was Pueblo style in most of its details but reminiscent of European Expressionism in total effect.

Trost and Trost specialized in reinforced concrete design—their Anson Mills Building in El Paso when completed in 1911 was one of the two or three largest reinforced concrete buildings anywhere—and Luhrs Tower is of concrete. Of fourteen stories with setbacks at the ninth and twelfth floors, in scale it is domestic rather than commercial, as befits an office building designed to attract tenants from the legal profession.[28] In its massing it owes much—as much as any skyscraper of the twenties—to Saarinen's *Chicago*

See pp. 85, 85.

Luhrs Tower, preliminary design II. (Arizona Collections, University Library, Arizona State University.)

Tribune design. The ornament, however, is Spanish, of sixteenth-century character around the entrance and in the store fronts, with candelabra colonnettes between the windows, but flattened and stylized in the Art Deco manner in the panels at the setbacks and around the tower, where terms with the physiognomy and in the dress of conquistadors supply a touch of whimsicality. Two alternative designs have survived and are reproduced here. In design I, the earlier, the tower is of fifteen stories (counting the machinery floor), turrets crowned with cupolas rise above the second setbacks, and the first two stories are treated as a unit. In design II the tower has been reduced by one story, the cupolas and their supporting structures have been suppressed to add another window bay to the outermost divisions of the elevation, and the height of the second setbacks has been increased one story to restore the space lost in the tower; the first story alone, with the entrance framed by pilasters and an entablature in place of the arch of design I, now forms the visual base of the building. The second design is the more harmonious of the two, and the executed design was evidently developed from it, the main changes being in the ornament of the upper stories and in the entrance, for which the arch has been reverted to.

The architects of the **Valley National Bank Annex** (originally the Valley Bank Professional Building), on the southeast corner of Central Avenue and Monroe Street, were Morgan, Walls and Clements of Los Angeles, whom we have had reason to mention earlier. Erected in 1931, it was the first steel-frame building in Phoenix. It was also, at $800,000, the most costly office building to that date. (The Title and Trust Building cost $650,000.) See pp. 86, 87.

While Luhrs Tower was principally for lawyers, the Valley Bank Professional Building was for the medical and dental professions. The bank and its offices, entered from Central Avenue, occupied the first two of its eleven floors; the third and fourth floors were for general commercial office use, the fifth was for laboratories and the remainder for physicians' and dentists' offices, the entrance to these being on Monroe Street; a garage was provided in the basement. The first two stories are faced with Indiana limestone, with a six-foot-high band of rose granite at street level; the piers above the third story are concrete-clad and the faceted spandrels were precast in concrete.

With its combination of broad and narrow piers, narrow window bays and off-center tower, the Valley National Bank Annex bears a marked resemblance to the same architects' Pellissier Building in Los Angeles, which was also completed in 1931. A remodeling of the top story has changed,

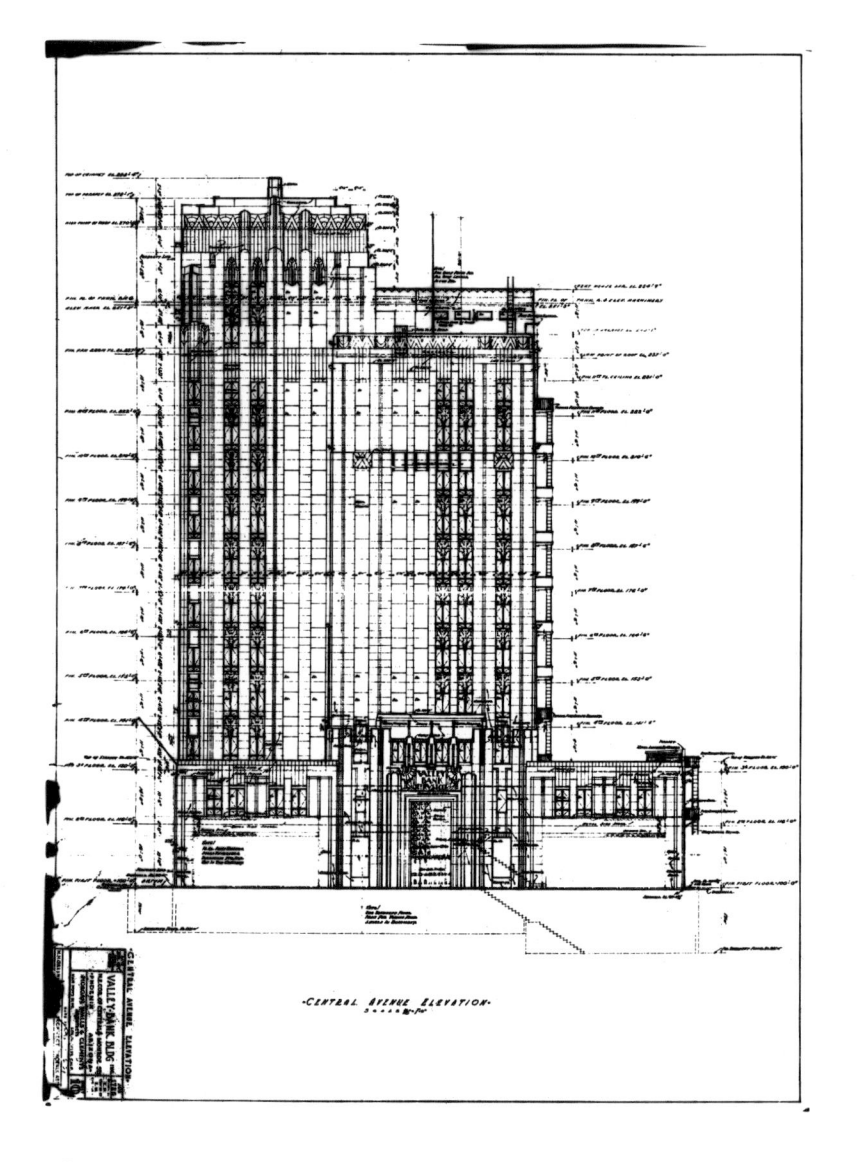

·CENTRAL AVENUE ELEVATION·

Valley National Bank Annex (Valley Bank Professional Building), Phoenix, Arizona, west elevation. (Valley National Bank.)

and spoiled, its silhouette, but the doors to the banking hall on Central Avenue and the elevator lobby on Monroe Street have escaped alteration. The latter, which is fifty feet long and twelve-and-a-half wide and high, is a fine Art Deco interior, if not as outstanding as the elevator lobby of the First Interstate Bank Building. Three kinds of pink marble are used on the walls and floor, with vert maurin at the base of the walls and framing the elevator doorways. The ceiling is divided into five compartments by beams with sunk panels containing abstract ornament. The elevator doors, with pierced foliated patterns, the directory, and the mailbox (a particularly handsome example of a feature on which Art Deco designers loved to lavish their skill) are of brass.

The **Winters Building,** formerly known as the Craig Building, on the See p. 88. southwest corner of First Avenue and Adams Street, dates from 1931. The building permit, for a Class B two-story office building to cost $65,000, was issued to R. W. Craig on February 24 that year; on June 2, according to the *Arizona Republic,* William Peper, the contractor, announced that construction was 90 percent complete; on July 26 the same newspaper noted that office space would be ready for occupancy "by first of next month or sooner," adding (rather mysteriously): "The decorated walk around the building has been cleared for pedestrian traffic." On August 28 a photograph of the building was incorporated in a montage of new Phoenix buildings in the *Republic.* But for all the interest the paper showed in it, it never saw fit to name the architects, who were Morgan, Walls, and Clements.

The Winters Building is a sophisticated design in which the problem of how to give consequence to a low building has been skillfully solved. The corner pavilion, with its two symmetrical (but not identical) facades, supplies a massive vertical feature where it is needed and balances the long horizontal of the Adams Street front; the stepping of the piers above the parapet, in conjunction with the faceting of the panels between them, gives the building a liveliness of silhouette that goes far to make up for its lack of height. The detail, too, is handled with sensitivity. The cast-concrete ornament on the upper part of the building is simple and bold; closer to eye level, over the store windows, are recessed panels of more elaborate scrollwork. Four original doorways remain in place, though only one, abutting the corner pavilion on Adams Street, still serves as an entrance; the other three are hidden in any distant view by an awning. They are all of the same design, of black marble sandblasted with a composition of chevrons over the lintel and an oval floral motif above. The store fronts are now plain and characterless—as a result, no doubt, of alterations costing $30,000 for which a building permit was issued in 1946.

TUCSON

See p. 89.

The **Reilly Funeral Home** at 102 East Pennington is at first sight a puzzling design. The broken silhouette, the piers and incised lines on the upper story, and the curtain-like ornaments on the west elevation are pure Art Deco. But the arched openings of the ground story, with rusticated keystones of all things—what of them? The explanation is that the Reilly Funeral Home was built circa 1909 and restyled twenty years later; originally, as the elevation reproduced here shows, it was more Romanesque than anything else. The architect of the building and for the restyling was Henry O. Jaastad. Born in Norway in 1872, Jaastad came to Tucson from Wisconsin in 1902 and worked as a carpenter until about 1908 when, having taken a course in architecture from the International Correspondence Schools, he started what soon became a highly successful practice as an architect. In later life he was mayor of Tucson for no less than seven successive terms. He worked in many styles, but the restyling of the Reilly Funeral Home seems to have been his only venture into Art Deco.[29]

FRONT ELEVATION

REAR ELEVATION

MORTUARY CHAPEL FOR JOHN L REILLY TUCSON AT.
Henry O. Jaastad, Arch.

08/1904

Reilly Funeral Home, Phoenix, Arizona, elevation before restyling. (Arizona
Architectural Archive, College of Architecture, University of Arizona.)

NEW MEXICO

ALBUQUERQUE

The architect of the **Albuquerque Indian Hospital,** unlike most of the architects whose work reflected regional character, was not a resident of the Southwest. Hans Stamm was chief of the Architectural Group of the Bureau of Indian Affairs in Washington. Built in 1934 as a tuberculosis sanatorium for Indian patients, the hospital was the first BIA structure to deviate from a standard design.[30] In response to Washington's reappraisal of the Indian cultures, Stamm researched the architecture of the Southwest.[31] As a result, the hospital has Pueblo characteristics in its pyramidal massing—inspired no doubt by Taos Pueblo—and stepped-pyramid decoration, the stepped pyramid being a motif found in Zuni fetish bowls and as a linear pattern in the pottery of other pueblos.

Seen in perspective, the south facade of the T-shaped structure gathers itself into a stepped-pyramid shape; two symmetrical stories rise to a third which is defined by piers clad with terra-cotta and embellished with stepped pyramids. The piers are repeated at the fourth story and accentuated by a projecting stepped-pyramid parapet, while the fifth-story setback has a stepped roof line. Finally, a tall chimney rises behind the penthouse, completing the pyramidal effect; like the parapets, it is finished with a fluted coping of green terra-cotta.

See pp. 90, 91.

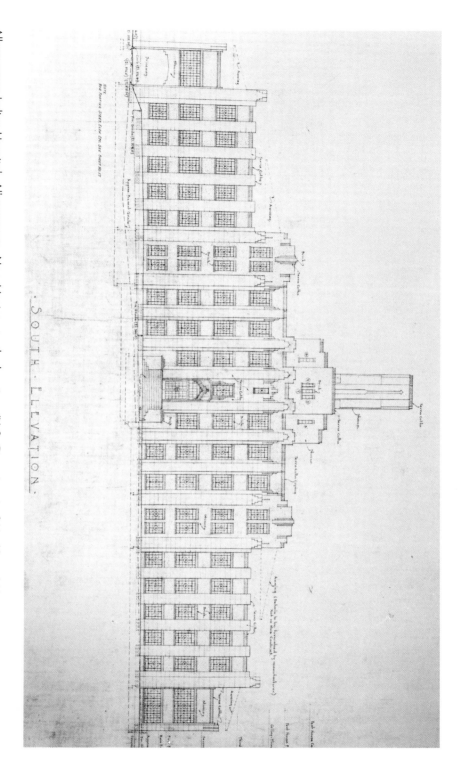

·SOUTH·ELEVATION·

Albuquerque Indian Hospital, Albuquerque, New Mexico, south elevation. (U.S. Department of Health and Human Services.)

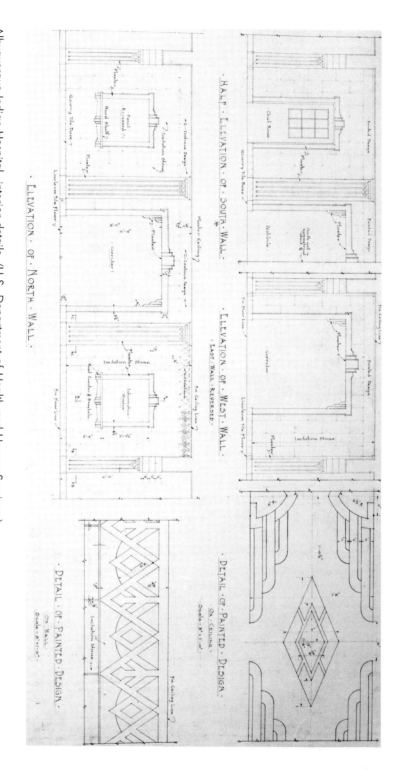

Albuquerque Indian Hospital, interior details. (U.S. Department of Health and Human Services.)

The stepped-pyramid motif is further elaborated in the entrance, where the double doors are surrounded by peach fluted terra-cotta encasing a narrow fluted band of green to form a stylized pyramid shape, repeated by windows of diminishing size above; the fourth-story window is outlined by a more intricate stepped pyramid. Soft blues, greens, reds, and mustard yellow make up the color scheme of the lobby, where painted pilasters, decorated with arrows, create the effect of pillars. The ceiling line is defined by a band of zigzags with alternating grounds of diamonds and thunder-birds, while the lintels of the doors and windows continue the stepped pyramid motif. A reference to the hospital's users appears in the form of a colored linoleum tile Indian head in the lobby's floor.

Using the stepped pyramid as a leitmotif, Stamm created in the Albuquerque Indian Hospital a coherent, elegantly modeled structure, modern by the standards of the thirties yet regional in flavor. The new wing (completed 1982), which obscures the original entrance and much of the first floor, was designed by Flatow, Moore, Bryan and Associates.

See pp. 92, 93. The **KiMo Theater** on the northeast corner of Central Avenue and Fifth Street was built in 1926–27. It is a quintessential example of Pueblo Deco, exhibiting a skillful fusion of Pueblo and Navajo motifs as decorative elements with Spanish mission form. Conceived and built by Oreste Bachechi, a successful Italian immigrant from Bagni di Lucca, in homage to the indigenous cultures of the Southwest, the theater was designed by Carl Boller with his brother and partner, Robert Boller.[32] Upon his engagement, Carl Boller was encouraged to travel about the region. Accompanied by the artist Carl Von Hassler, he traveled extensively, guided by a fur and Indian jewelry trader, Schmidt.[33] In this manner Boller assimilated aspects of the Pueblo, Navajo, and Spanish cultures.[34]

The building he designed as a result is a brick structure (reinforced with steel) characterized by the massive forms of Spanish Pueblo Revival architecture. Terra-cotta ornament inspired by Pueblo pottery and textiles, Navajo mythology, and Spanish decoration is liberally applied. The facade is tripartite, the central section being narrower than the others and slightly set back. Originally the east and west bays corresponded with the storefronts below. Above the third-story windows is a band of shields alternating with spindles. Shields correspond with piers and cascade down in diminishing steps composed of triangles, chevrons, and stylized feathers in a manner reminiscent of the *faldoncito* of the Mexican Baroque. Pueblo and Navajo motifs are applied to the shields, the Pueblo rain motif which resembles a

KiMo Theater, Albuquerque, New Mexico, perspective from the southwest. (Orie Bachechi.)

cumulus cloud alternating with the Navajo directional symbol and a bird form inspired by Acoma pottery.[35] A running stepped pyramid links the spindles and frames the upper portion of the shields.[36] The elaborate spindles with finials are composed of vegetable forms. The spandrels occurring between the second- and third-floor windows contain mixtilinear corbeled arches with a background of colored terra-cotta tiles; window lintels have a relief checkerboard pattern, another motif derived from Pueblo culture.[37] Spindlework transoms over the storefront windows, long obscured by a later marquee, have been revealed again by the recent restoration.[38]

The band of terra-cotta shields is continued over the three windows on the west elevation. Below the sills of these windows are inverted stepped pyramids. Stout pilasters with terra-cotta capitals composed of frets and inverted volutes divide the first-story display windows; below the capitals are stylized Kachina masks in colored tile. Inverted stepped pyramids appear again below the false inset balconies which relieve the massive quality of this elevation. False vigas project from the balconies and above each of them are two shields joined by a more typical Art Deco ornament, running zigzags in red, white, and blue terra-cotta tiles.

The interior of the KiMo is no less richly decorated than the exterior. The entry opens directly into the lobby; the mezzanine, running the length of the lobby, is reached by stairs, with balusters of wrought iron in the form of stylized water fowl, at each end. Murals by Von Hassler depicting the Spanish myth of the "Seven Cities of Cibola" decorate the walls leading up to the mezzanine and that of the mezzanine itself. Terra-cotta buffalo skulls—a reference to the Buffalo Dance at Taos Pueblo—illuminate the theater and lobby with eerie effect. During the 1930s a wealth of miscellaneous details reinforced the theater's Indian theme. Navajo rugs lay on the lobby floor, and Pueblo pottery was scattered about. The concrete beams were painted to simulate wood vigas and embellished with painted thunderbirds, stylized butterflies, and geometrical motifs. Upon entering the auditorium, one would have been overwhelmed by the ornate proscenium arch. Alterations over the years have reduced the original impact.

The exterior of the KiMo Theater has a rhythmic quality created by the ascending repetition of stepped pyramids and corbeled arches. While its Indian-inspired ornament was transformed by the Art Deco aesthetic,[39] the intent to "remain faithful to Indian principles" is clearly visible. At the same time Spanish elements in the volumes and scattered decorative devices contribute to make this building what Oreste Bachechi intended it to be—

an architectural tribute to the cultures of the Southwest: Pueblo, Navajo, and Spanish.

The **Maisel Building** (currently the Ney Trading Post, although the building retains its original name) at 510 Central Avenue, S.W., was designed by John Gaw Meem and built in 1937. The leading Spanish Pueblo-style architect in New Mexico, Meem designed three Art Deco buildings, and one which has Art Deco elements—Scholes Hall on the University of New Mexico campus.[40] Meem's notes from one of his initial conversations with the client, Maurice M. Maisel, stated that he (Maisel) was "not content with the usual conventional Indian thing." "It was agreed finally that my preliminary study was to be along the lines of a strictly modern structure using where necessary Indian symbols."[41] Maisel gave Meem a photograph of Schaver's in Los Angeles (a building that we are unable to identify), requesting that a similar display area be designed but with angular instead of curved forms.[42]

See pp. 94, 95.

The result of Meem's sketches is a recessed lobby forming a T-shaped display area; the display windows are semihexagonal at the corners. A mural designed and supervised by Olive Rush forms a frieze above the display windows and extends across the facade. Depicting various aspects of Pueblo and Navajo ceremonial life, this was one of the first murals to be painted by Indian artists outside the American Indian Art Institute in Santa Fe.[43] It introduces an element of authenticity rare in Pueblo Deco design. Pablita Velarde, Pop Chalee, and Harrison Begay were among the nine artists who worked on it, each being responsible for given panels.[44] Several of the images differ only slightly in pictorial content and technique from the murals which have appeared since prehistory in ritual context in pueblo culture, such as those at Awatobi.

Above and on either side of the entrance an aluminum molding forms stepped diamonds, a motif encountered in Navajo textiles during the second half of the nineteenth century, when the famed Chief's Blanket predominated. Below the display windows is black Carrara glass, etched in silver with a sinuous, faintly floral motif which bears some resemblance to stylized plant forms appearing on Pueblo pottery or the Avanyu on San Ildefonso pottery, with Spanish elements in the twisted rope and partial rosette forms. The terrazzo floor is embellished with a stylized thunderbird of crushed turquoise and coral embedded with silver dollars and pesos, which are also used to form the trader's name. A feature of the interior is a balcony

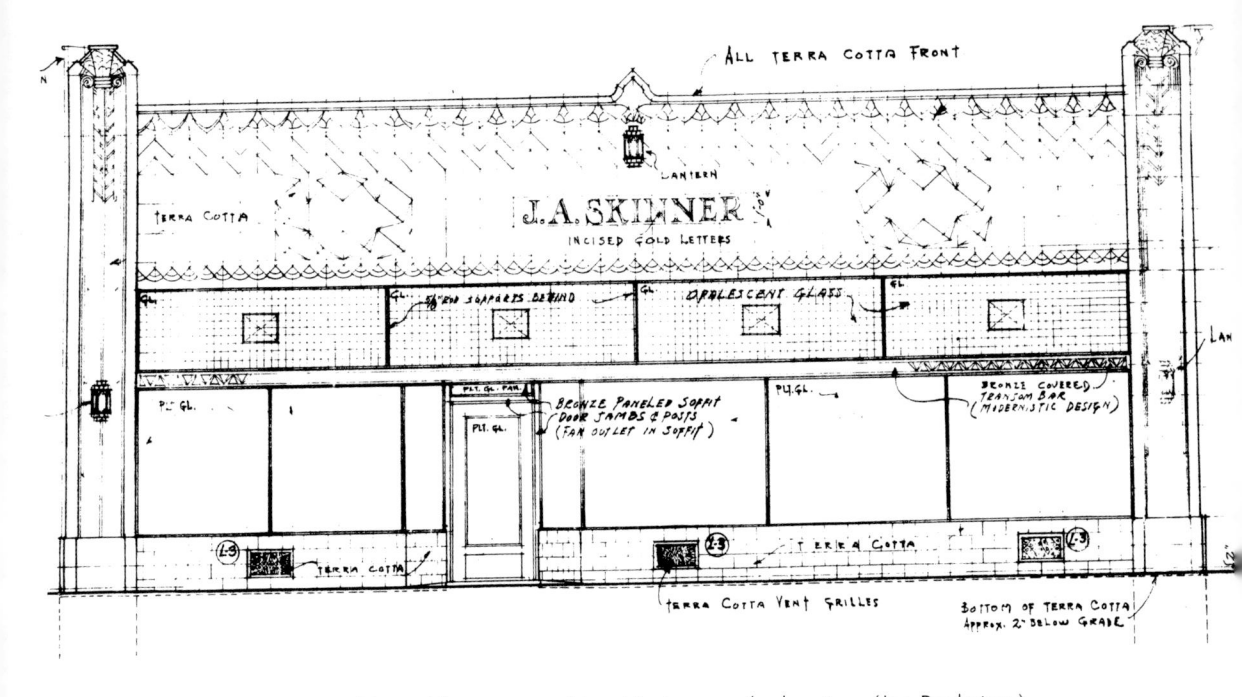

Skinner Building, Albuquerque, New Mexico, north elevation. (Joe Boehning.)

from which tourists could watch the Indian jewelers employed by Maisel's at work in the basement.

The architect of the **Skinner Building,** on the southwest corner of Eighth Street and Central Avenue, was A. W. Boehning. Having moved to the Southwest to treat his tuberculosis, Boehning worked as a draftsman for Trost and Trost until 1924, when he opened his own office.[45] In the Skinner Building, designed in 1931 as a grocery store, he employed neutral terra-cotta as incised tiles, molded forms, and simple cladding. Terra-cotta-clad piers flank the facade and punctuate the west elevation, rising above the parapet. The elaboration of decoration on them increases with their height. Stepped incised lines lead into a vertical herringbone, culminating in a truncated pyramid with incised decoration and reversed volutes forming a stylized papyrus motif. The areas between the piers on the facade and west elevation are composed of four bands of incised terra-cotta. The upper band along the parapet consists of a running ogive alternating with a ground filled with scallops; below it is a running zigzag. Below that is a band of plain square tiles, while the lowest band is a variation on the parapet band, with a running zigzag instead of the ogive and every other triangular space filled with quarter circles. Above the display windows a running band of stepped diamonds in opalescent glass is evidence of the architect's knowledge of Navajo textiles;[46] the bronze transom bar below it is ornamented with opposing triangles. Boehning demonstrates in the Skinner Building an interest in overall decoration while knowledgeably inserting regional references.

See pp. 96, 97.

Wright's Trading Post (the Office Furniture Mart), at 616 Central Avenue, N.W., shows the kind of imaginative adaptation of Indian motifs that is found in the work of John Gaw Meem. However, Meem's office files and records provide no indication that he was responsible for the design, which remains unattributed. The facade above the inset entry is composed of three horizontal sections. The central section is rendered with white stucco, originally lettered with the trading post's name;[47] above it louver-like vertical panels reflect the sunlight of the Southwest. It is the lowest section that gives the facade most of its decorative interest. It is faced with small turquoise glass tiles; in the center and at each end are aluminum fans and below it is a narrow band of louvers like those of the uppermost section but smaller and more delicate. The cumulative effect of the detail on this portion of the facade at a distance is of Pueblo turquoise and silver jewelry, on a vastly magnified scale. Black and turquoise glazed tiles surround the display windows and entrance.

See p. 98.

CLOVIS

See pp. 99,
100, 101.

The **Clovis Hotel** was built in 1928–32. Its architect, Robert Merrell, graduated from Texas A & M in 1920 and subsequently attended the Ecole des Beaux-Arts. On his return from France he entered the employment of the Moody Cotton Company in Galveston, for whom he supervised the construction of the Clovis Hotel; after its completion he settled permanently in Clovis, opening his own practice there.

For a short period this eleven-story hotel, which bears Merrell's imprint in the decorative cast aluminum and concrete, was the tallest building in New Mexico. The west and north entrances are sheltered by cantilevers with decorative aluminum details. Cast-concrete piers are decorated with elaborate floral motifs and form a stepped pyramid where they end at the second floor; four Plains Indian warriors' heads project above the ninth-story parapet. A setback penthouse rises another two stories, but is unembellished. Inside, Indian influence appears in wrought-iron lighting fixtures with arrow motifs, and in earth-colored tiles. Many of the original fixtures have been lost as a result of the numerous sales of the hotel since the Moody Corporation sold it in 1965.

See p. 101.

The **Curry County Courthouse** was built in 1936; its architect was Robert Merrell. The facade consists of a central entrance pavilion flanked by setback wings. The rectangular projecting entrance is surrounded by grooved terra-cotta and panels with a vertical herringbone motif, repeated on a smaller scale on the second story. Above the doorway is the Zia sun symbol, colored orange; the same motif appears on the spandrels between the first- and second-story windows. A coping at the second-floor level is ornamented with a running band of frets, with chevrons in the center and at the corners. Although this building reveals something of Merrell's decorative facility, it is more in evidence in the Roosevelt County Courthouse at Portales.

See p. 102.

The **James M. Bickley School,** another work of Robert Merrell, was built in 1932. It has a rounded central entrance, flanked by two long wings which curve slightly. The transom windows over the entrance are covered with an aluminum grille with a variation on the stepped-diamond motif. The coping which caps the central portion of the red brick structure is grooved terra-cotta. The red-brick wings contain separate entries, each flanked by panels of cast concrete decorated with a less stylized diamond motif, while another, an elongated version of the same motif is employed in the transom grilles.

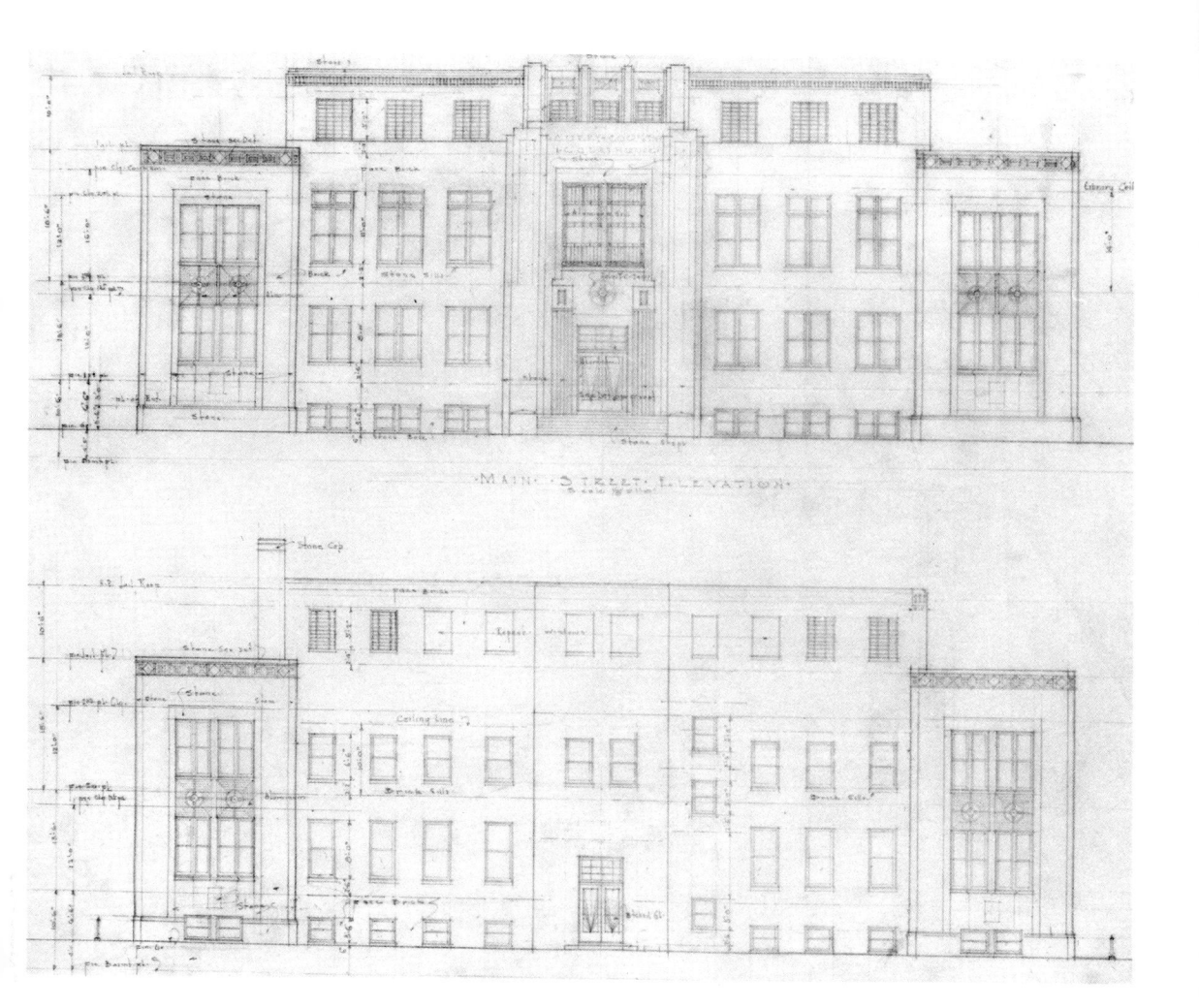

·MAIN·STREET·ELEVATION·

Curry County Courthouse, Clovis, New Mexico, Main Street elevation. (Warren Pendleton.)

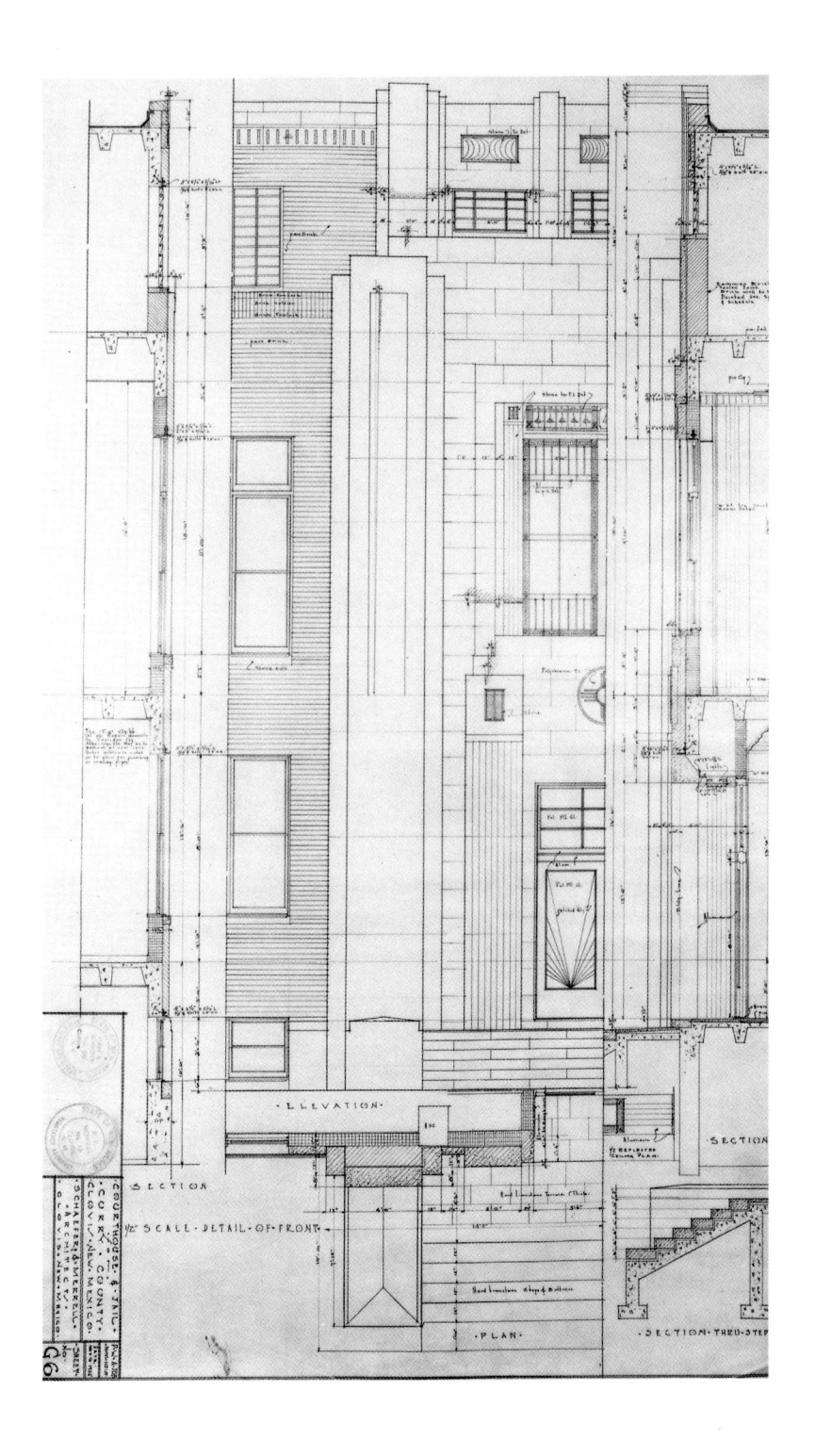

MOUNTAINAIR

The **Shaffer Hotel** is as much a product of the cultural influences of the Southwest as of the Saturday architect, Clem "Pop" Shaffer, who built it. It is the 1929 addition that manifests Pueblo Deco characteristics.[48] Containing the dining room and additional accommodations on the second floor, this frame and masonry section is distinguished by its incised stucco work. The facade is bilaterally symmetrical with four Navajo directional symbols—two on each side—flanking the second-story windows. Vigas project at first- and second-story ceiling levels; above the lower vigas there is a row of recessed squares, colored alternately orange and turquoise, and above the upper ones a similar row of turquoise squares. More incised stucco work embellishes the parapet line, with long recessed rectangles and, below them, orange triangles forming a zigzag. The original transom windows above the entrance and first-floor windows are of opalescent glass, spelling out *dining room* and ornamented with thunderbird motifs.

See p. 103.

Although the Shaffer Hotel addition is hardly a major work of architecture, the incised stucco work—a technique rarely employed elsewhere—lifts it above the ordinary.

PORTALES

The **Roosevelt County Courthouse,** designed by Robert Merrell, was completed in 1937; it was constructed with Public Works Administration funds. It is in poor condition externally; the aluminum grillwork and spandrels give an indication of its original appearance. The entrance is spectacularly high, rising three stories and flanked by layered piers. The aluminum grille over the transom windows is molded with a thunderbird motif alternating with diamonds. Projecting above the transom are aluminum spandrels with an elongated Zia sun symbol between the second- and third-story windows. A cast concrete frieze above this section depicts men on horses riding across the desert, in reference to the county's cattle industry. Across this frieze run medallions, cast in the shape of the Zia sun symbol, the state symbol of New Mexico. At the fourth story the piers rise above the parapet.

See p. 103.

Facing page: Curry County Courthouse, detail of Main Street elevation. (Warren Pendleton.)

RATON

See pp.
104, 105.

The **Colfax County Courthouse** was built in 1936. It was designed by William C. Townes of Amarillo, architect of the (earlier) courthouse there; construction was supervised by R. W. Vorhees of Roswell. It ranks with the very different Cochise County Courthouse at Bisbee, Arizona, as one of the two best Art Deco courthouses in the Southwest. Its five-part facade, of brick and cast stone, steps up from three-story wings to a five-story center, from which a three-part entrance pavilion projects. By advancing each section of the facade and of the entrance pavilion slightly in front of its outer neighbor—with the result that there are five different wall planes— the structure has been given a dynamic centripetal movement horizontally as well as vertically, while the sense of mass has been enhanced at the same time. A deep band of cast stone defines the upper part of the central section of the facade and forms a border to the brickwork against which the entrance pavilion is set; in it are two medallions containing reliefs, one of a farmer with a scythe, the other of a miner wielding a pick. The importance of cattle is acknowledged with relief steers' heads on the entrance pavilion and the county brands, in zinc, over the doors. The Zia sun symbol embellishes copings and window lintels.

WEST TEXAS

AMARILLO

The **Kress Store** was designed by the Amarillo architect R. R. Rowe in 1932. See p. 106.
A rectangular loft structure of two stories, it is clad in buff brick with terra-
cotta details. An ornamented cantilever extends the length of the facade;
the two entries are recessed. Patterned brickwork contrasts with the molded
terra-cotta lintels of the second-story windows, both on the facade and on
the north elevation. Panels of brightly colored terra-cotta, each depicting
a large yellow flower in a latticed pot, occur at intervals above the second-
story windows. The Kress building in Amarillo is much less extravagant than
those in Phoenix and El Paso, no doubt because Amarillo had not develoepd
to a comparable size by this period.

The **Potter County Courthouse** was built in 1930–32, at a cost of nearly See p. 107.
$315,000. The architects were Townes, Lightfoot and Funk. Though with
only eight stories far from qualifying as a skyscraper, like many courthouses
of its time it owes much to skyscraper design in its massing with setbacks
and the unbroken verticals of the piers of the central tower; unlike most of
them, it is double fronted, with a triple-arched entrance pavilion on each
front. The structure is reinforced concrete, the cladding cast stone. As in
the other courthouses in this book, the architects have been at pains to give
the building a local or regional flavor through the use of sculptural (here
cast-stone) reliefs, with a composition of prickly pear cactus over the main

White and Kirk Department Store, Amarillo, Texas, perspective from the Southwest. (Amarillo Public Library.)

Facing page: Xerox Building (Paramount Theater), Amarillo, Texas, south and west elevations. (Terrence Donne Associates.)

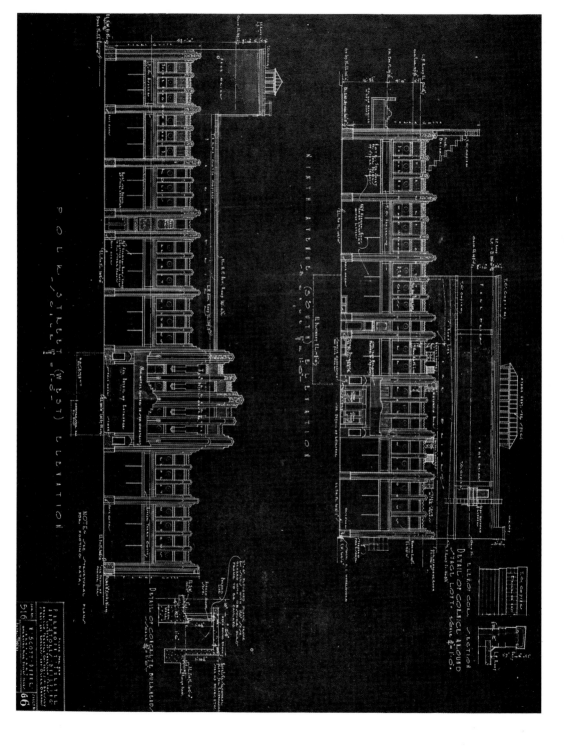

entrance and figures of frontiersmen and Indians high on the piers of the tower. Handsome though it is, in a comparison with Townes's Colfax County Courthouse at Raton, New Mexico, the Potter County Courthouse will be adjudged by most the loser.

See p. 109.

The **White and Kirk Department Store,** at 516 South Polk, was built in 1938. Its architect, Guy A. Carlander, received his architectural training with the Santa Fe railroad. While employed in their Chicago office he designed the Atchison, Topeka & Santa Fe hospitals in Albuquerque, Los Angeles, and Topeka, and traveled extensively in the Southwest to supervise construction and engineering. In 1920, at a time of accelerated construction due to discoveries of gas and oil, he opened his own practice in Amarillo. Until the 1930s his designs were influenced by the Spanish revival, although his intrest in details and textures was evident. His personal style began to emerge with the Amarillo College Administration Building and the Gymnasium of 1936 through 1939. The White and Kirk Department Store is the best example of his work during this period. A steel-frame structure, it is faced with buff brick. Its rectangular form is offset by a circulation tower of stepped pylons. Terra-cotta spandrels separate the second-, third-, and fourth-story windows; an overlapping diamond pattern fills the spandrels with a texture contrasting with the brick. The fourth-story windows are in the form of a truncated stepped pyramid. Between the first and second stories occurs a frieze of terra-cotta, incised with yucca plants in bloom and a geometrical motif (as Mary Carlander remembers, first carved in Ivory soap).

See p. 110.

The **Xerox Building,** originally the Paramount Theater, at 817 South Polk, was built in 1932. It was designed by W. Scott Dunne, a Dallas architect well known for his theater designs. Although it is well maintained, what in its day was the most lavish theater in Amarillo has lost much of its original character through remodeling. Where the marquee once was, the entrance pavilion rises above the parapet; both pavilion and parapet have a zigzag silhouette. Open bays separate the structural piers, which are of compound section with black marble bases. The cladding is terra-cotta, molded and colored above the second-story windows and at the parapet line, with ornamentation that includes fluting, fans, zigzags, and elaborate floral motifs. The tops of the piers, which rise above the parapet, are pointed and decorated with red and green foliate reliefs. Floral designs occur between the windows, at one time of etched glass but now of a dark glass which destroys the building's unity and lightness.

EL PASO

The **Bassett Tower,** on the northeast corner of East Texas Avenue and South Stanton Street, was completed to the design of Henry Trost in 1930, within weeks of the same architect's Luhrs Tower in Phoenix.[50] If any two buildings could be described as twins, they are the Luhrs and Bassett towers. They are not identical twins, however. The fenestration and system of setbacks, at the ninth and twelfth floors, is the same in both, but Bassett is a story higher than Luhrs. Then unlike the latter it is faced with exposed brick, which gives it a sharper, clean-cut quality. In the spandrels bricks project from the face of the wall to provide texture and a play of light and shade— a treatment to be traced, perhaps, to the Expressionist school of Hamburg in the early twenties. The entrance aedicule, which embraces the central windows of the second story, is of limestone on a granite plinth, as are also the piers between the storefronts, which have a limestone fascia with inset marble panels. The ornament is concentrated at the setbacks and around the top of the tower. Of brick with panels of marble, it is of greater salience than the ornament of Luhrs Tower; at a distance it modifies the silhouette of the building instead of being absorbed into its mass. It is also of completely different character, Art Deco of the most abstract kind without any admixture of Spanish. The lobby, which is twenty-four feet square, shows Trost at his most classicizing; it has a floor of various marbles, pilasters of verd antique in the corners, and a coffered ceiling. The bronze grille over the entrance and the elevator doors contribute much to the sumptuous effect.

See pp. 111, 112, 113, 114, 115.

Although it does not have the immediate appeal that color gives to Luhrs Tower, the Bassett Tower, with its architectonic ornament and better-managed entrance, is the stronger design. Tradition has it that the head carved in stone over the entrance is Trost's own. If that is true, he chose his monument well.

The **Kress Store** was built to the design of Edward Sibbert, in 1937–38. Planned as an L with its base running through the block from Oregon Street to Mesa Avenue, it has three street elevations, those toward Oregon and Mills streets meeting in an eighty-foot tower while the third, on Mesa Avenue, abuts the Roberts-Banner Building (Henry Trost, 1910), which together with a smaller store fills up the rectangular space defined by the L.

See pp. 116, 117, 118, 119.

The Kress Store is a *tour de force* in the use of terra-cotta, which is employed, in two different shades, for the facing of the walls and also,

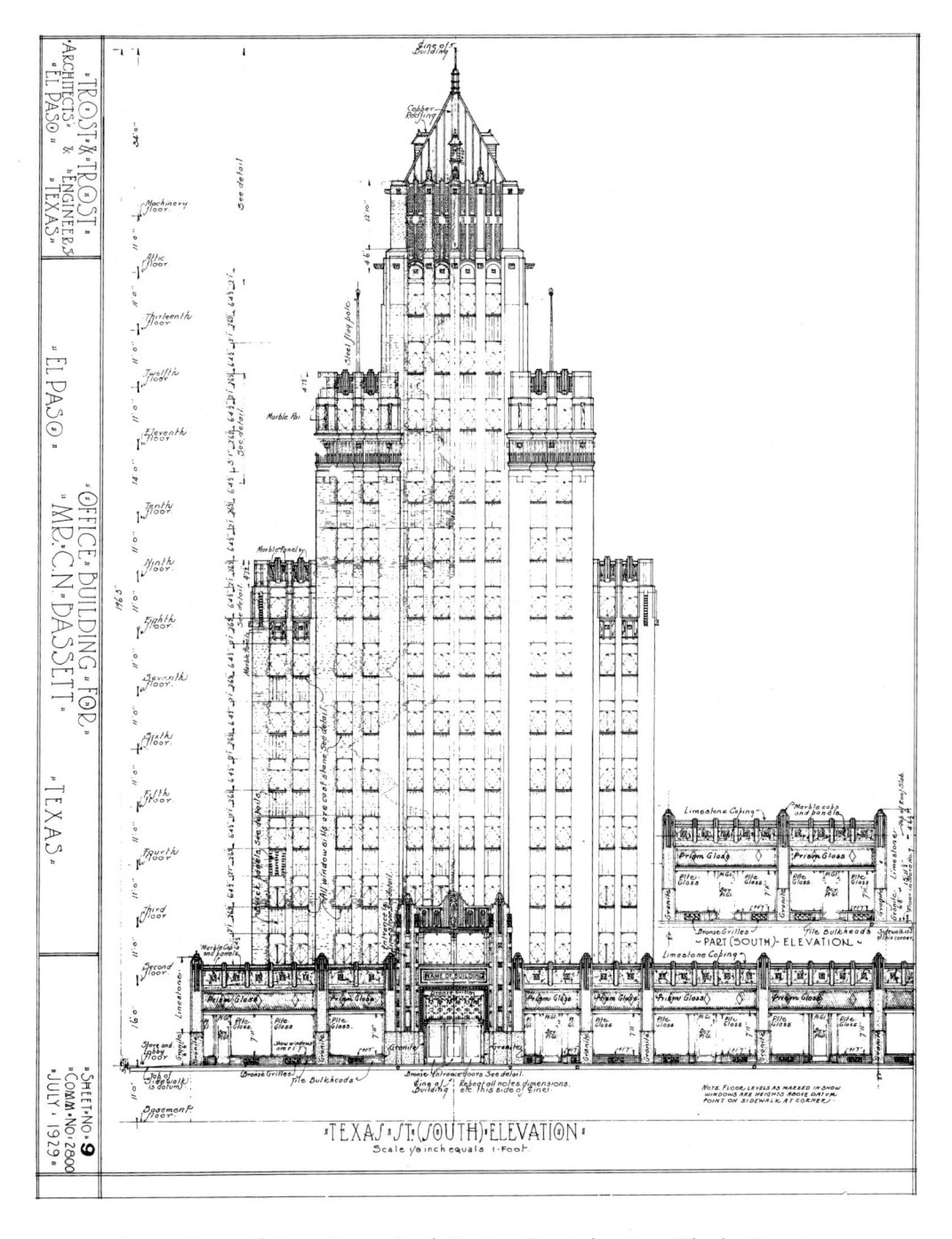

Bassett Tower, El Paso, Texas, South Stanton Street elevation. (Charles Bassett Hammond.)

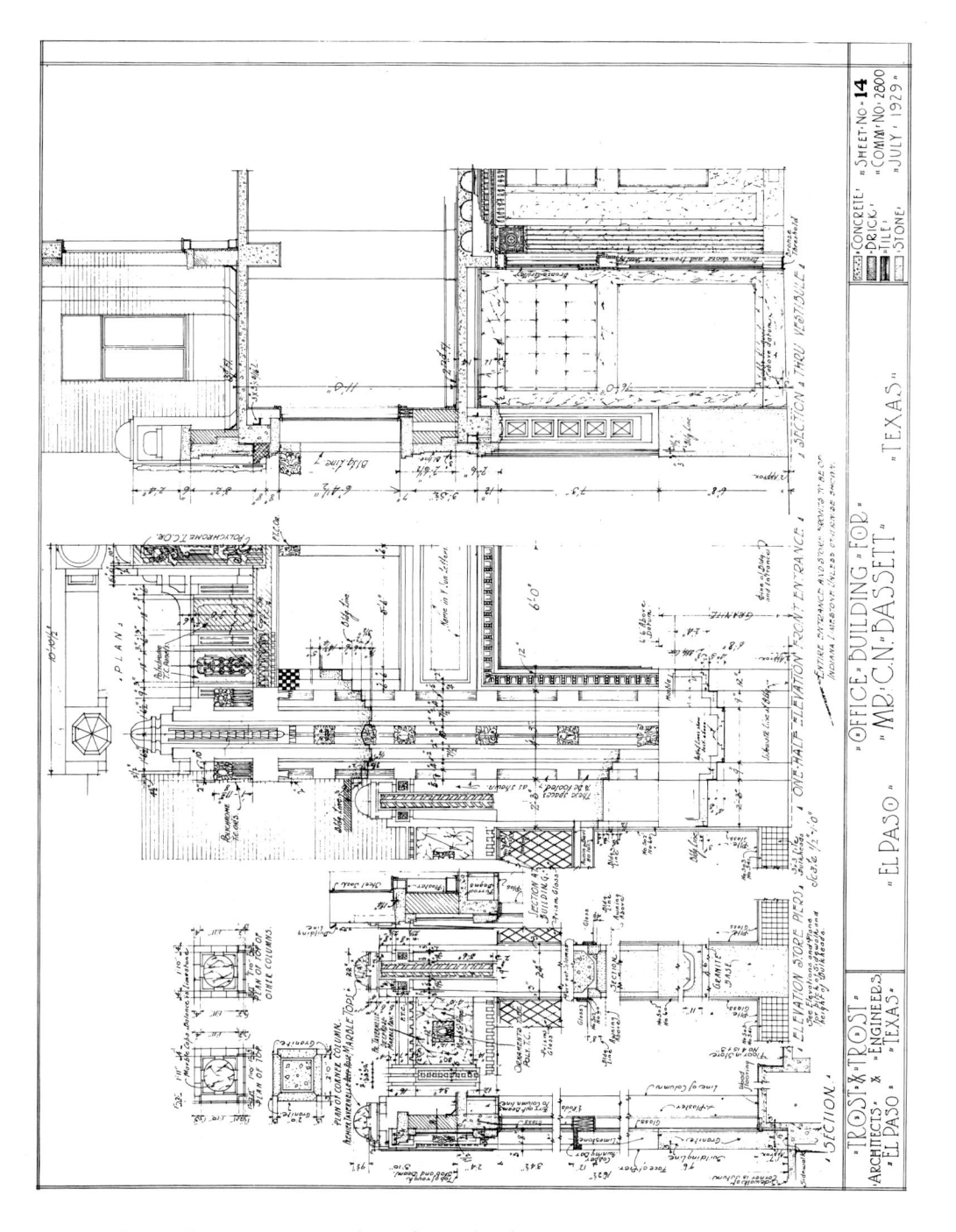

Bassett Tower, entrance and storefront, details.

Kress Store, El Paso, Texas, Mesa Avenue elevation. (Genesco Incorporated.)

Kress Store, Mills Street elevation and details. (Genesco Incorporated.)

in red, blue, green, and gold, for all the ornament. As for the character of that ornament, for the most part it is generically Moorish—not scholarly but not undisciplined either.[51] (One suspects that there was a copy of Owen Jones' *Grammar of Ornament* in Sibbert's office, though comparison of the plates with the architect's drawings has failed to reveal any direct borrowings.) The pattern of the tiles flanking the store's name over the Oregon Street entrance derives from the plan of a Moorish patio or enclosed garden, which is divided into quadrants with a low tile fountain in the center. There are Spanish touches too, in the iron balconies and in the mirador-like top stage of the tower with its terra-cotta latticework. Yet in the final analysis the Kress Store is incontrovertibly Art Deco; let anyone who doubts it study the Mesa Avenue elevation, where the two shades of terra-cotta are used to speed the eye's ascent to the broken skyline.

An admirable building in itself, the Kress Store is also an element of the greatest importance in the townscape of El Paso. Its contiguity to the Roberts-Banner Building has already been mentioned; on Oregon Street across the corner of San Jacinto Plaza stands Trost's great Anson Mills Building, defaced with brown paint and reflecting glass but still a powerful presence. Although it would seem that the tower of the Kress Store was suggested by the fact that its predecessor on the site had a tower, one feels that Sibbert must have taken the proximity of the Mills Building into account. In any case the two buildings complement each other by being so different, much as the Erechtheum and the Parthenon complement each other. Fortunately, the El Paso Kress seems to be in no danger at present of suffering the fate that has overtaken its cousin in Phoenix. To enter it is to take several steps back in time, into a busy five-and-ten in the 1930s.

NOTES

1. C. M. Price, "The Panama-California Exposition," *Architectural Record* 37 (March 1915): 242.

2. Ibid., 238.

3. T. E. Sanford, *The Architecture of the Southwest* (New York: W. W. Norton and Co., 1950), 249, 274.

4. Not all were favorably impressed. In January 1926 a writer in the *Architectural Forum* exulted: "Les Arts Decoratifs are no more! . . . This bastard offspring of anaemic artisanship and efficient salesmanship was not fit to live. We buried it on the banks of the Seine." E. H. Hostache, "Reflections on the Exposition des Arts Décoratifs," *Architectural Forum* 44 (January 1926): 11–16.

5. The adjective is H. S. Bradshaw's, in his report on the architecture of the exhibition published by the British Board of Trade in *Reports of the Present Position and Tendencies of the Industrial Arts as indicated at the International Exhibition of Modern Decorative and Industrial Arts, Paris, 1925*. Neither the Pavillon de l'Esprit Nouveau, nor the Russian Pavilion is anywhere mentioned in this volume. For a brief account of the exhibition, see *1925: A Personal Recollection of the Paris Exhibition* by F. Scarlett and M. Townley (London: Academy Editions, 1975).

6. In M. Tafuri and F. Dal Co, *Modern Architecture* (New York: Harry N. Abrams, 1979), an apartment block by Pierre Patout is the subject of two illustrations, and L. A. Boileau is named as a member of the committee that supervised the building of the Palais de Chaillot in 1937.

7. For a brief summing up of the differences between Sullivan's ornament and

Art Nouveau ornament, see M. Whiffen, *American Architecture Since 1780: A Guide to the Styles* (Cambridge, Mass.: MIT Press, 1969), 195.

8. E. J. Kahn, "Sources of Inspiration," *Architecture* 60 (November 1929): 252.

9. H. R. Hitchcock, *Architecture: Nineteenth and Twentieth Centuries* (Baltimore, Md.: Penguin Books, 1958), 360.

10. "Some Industrial Buildings by George C. Nimmons," *Architectural Record* 38 (August 1915): 231.

11. By C. Robinson and M. H. Bletter in *Skyscraper Style: Art Deco New York* (New York: Oxford University Press, 1975).

12. J. S. Cahill, "The Telephone Building, San Francisco," *Architecture* 53 (February 1926): 53–54.

13. For example, James W. Plachek, in the facades of whose Berkeley Public Library (1931) chevron ornament above the windows is combined with Mayan sgraffito panels below them and Mayan carvings crowning the buttress-pylons.

14. A. C. Bossom, "America's National Architecture," *American Architect* 128 (July 24, 1925): 77–83.

15. M. Whiffen, *American Architecture Since 1780,* p. 240.

16. *Kem Weber: The Moderne in Southern California 1920 through 1941* (Santa Barbara, Calif.: Art Galleries, University of California, Santa Barbara, 1969).

17. J. Stirling, "Architectural Aims and Influences," *R.I.B.A. Journal* (September 1980): n.p.

18. El Navajo Hotel was designed in 1915 with E. A. Harrison as architect of record but not built until 1923. Coulter reproduced otherwise transient Navajo sand paintings (made with dry pigments) in large-scale panels. Motifs from these sand paintings were repeated in the woodwork, wrought-iron work, and lighting fixtures. At the dedication of the hotel, Navajo medicine men blessed the structure and its sand paintings, which are traditionally produced during curing ceremonies and then erased. "El Navajo Hotel Brings Sand Paintings into the Pathway of Tourist Travel," *Albuquerque Journal* (New Mexico), May 27, 1923.

19. R. Pare, editor, *Court House: A Photographic Document* (New York: Horizon Press, 1978), 243.

20. Whether Meaney knew it or not, the truncated pyramid occurring in a band is symbolic of the cloud motif from the Navajo sand painting, *The Mountain Chant.* "Navajo Sand Paintings as Decorative Motives," *El Palacio* 14 (June 15, 1923), no. 12.

21. Much of the information in this and the following paragraphs is derived from a manuscript memoir by Albert McArthur in the possession of Warren McArthur, III.

22. Letter by Charles McArthur to *Arizona Highways,* quoted by Dorothy Goebel, "Speech Zeroes in on Biltmore Design," *Phoenix Gazette*, section C (March 4, 1976): 1–2.

23. In shape the concrete units are tiles rather than blocks, being little more than two inches thick. Each wall consists of two skins of these units, reinforced vertically and horizontally with steel rods and tied together by steel struts. The use of standard units made it possible to dispense with dimensions on the working drawings, and a process that might be called building-by-numbers was employed.

24. Sketch by Albert McArthur in the possession of Warren McArthur, Jr.

25. Extensive additions have been made to the Arizona Biltmore in recent years, beginning with a ballroom by Flatow, Moore, Bryan and Fairburn in 1969. After a fire in 1973 the building was restored by Taliesin Associated Architects and largely refurnished from designs made by Wright for use elsewhere. Two wings were added, northeast of the original building, in 1975 and 1979, a conference center to the west in 1979, and a court to the north in 1981, all by Taliesin Associated Architects.

26. The clients maintained that to decorate the ceiling would be a waste of money because on entering a building people never looked up. (Conversation with the architect, February 10, 1982.) According to the *Arizona Republic,* describing the building on the occasion of its official opening on January 31, 1931, the ceiling was to be decorated in silver and black.

27. For his life and work, see L. C. and J. M. F. Engelbrecht, *Henry C. Trost, Architect of the Southwest* (El Paso, Texas: El Paso Public Library Association, 1981).

28. On April 28, 1928, H. Jerome Toy of H. Jerome Toy and Company, Promoters and Financial Agents, wrote George Luhrs: "I believe there is an opening on your corner for a Law building, being so close to the new court house. I would suggest that all attorneys in Phoenix be lined up before they get located in the Security Building—I have a live man who could handle this angle of the work successfully, if you would care to make use of him." Bids were advertised for on February 26, 1929; the contract price was $208,275. Luhrs papers, Arizona Collection, University Library, Arizona State University.

29. There is a large collection of Jaastad drawings in the Arizona Architectural Archive of the College of Architecture, University of Arizona.

30. National Register of Historic Places Inventory: nomination form prepared by S. V. Dewitt, 1980.

31. Ibid.

32. Robert Boller is the better-known brother and claimed credit for the KiMo Theater in the *American Architects Directory* (New York: R. R. Bowker Co., 1955); however, according to Oreste Bachechi's grandson, Orie Bachechi, Carl Boller was the principal designer. The only existing copy of an original drawing is signed by Carl Boller. Conversation between Carla Breeze and Orie Bachechi, April 1, 1982.

33. Ibid.

34. Perhaps Boller's experiences were supplemented by articles appearing during this period, for example, A. F. Simmons, "Pueblo—A Native American Architecture," *House and Garden* (April 1922): 52–54.

35. There are several possible sources for Boller's use of the shield motif. According to Orie Bachechi, Pablo Abeita of Isleta Pueblo acted as a design consultant, but whether he contributed actual drawings or simply advised after motifs were chosen is undetermined. In the Indian ceremonial parades held during the 1920s in Albuquerque, decorated shields with numerous appendages (more typically encountered as shield covers among the Plains tribes) were carried by participants. A Fred Harvey publication entitled *The Hopi Sun Shield: Its Meaning* demonstrates the interest at the time in this motif. The most probable source seems to be Inez B. Westlake, the interior designer who worked with Boller on the KiMo Theater. As the interior designer of Trost's Hotel Franciscan, she adapted Pueblo motifs for the interior decoration. Photographs reveal that the medallions designed by Westlake (inspired by the Hopi potter, Nampaya) bear a great resemblance to those used on and in the KiMo, and similarly, are repeated in bands or borders. R. Henderson, "The Spanish-Indian Tradition in Interior Decoration," *Architectural Record* 61 (Jan.–June, 1927).

36. The stepped pyramid is a motif associated with rain and consequently with fertility symbolism. F. Boas, *Primitive Art* (New York: Dover Publications, 1955), 120.

37. The checkerboard motif often occurs on kilts worn by ceremonial dancers, and symbolizes corn.

38. H. S. Hoshour, *Historic Structure Report of the KiMo* (Santa Fe: Historic Preservation Bureau, 1980), 11.

39. "America's Foremost Indian Theater," Program of Events for Ceremonial Opening of the KiMo Theater, Valiant Printing Co., 1927.

40. Meem designed a second trading post influenced by Art Deco for the Maisel family. From extant photographs, it appears to have lacked the sophistication of the existing Maisel Building. The third Art Deco building Meem designed was the unexecuted Simms Professional Building. Rough drawings document its development. Sketches dated February 4, 1937 outline a ten-story building with the windows grouped between narrow piers; the tenth floor was decorated with herringbone patterns formed of alternating vertical and horizontal brick facings. The recessed entry was of distinctly Territorial character, with an elaborately carved pedimented lintel. In subsequent drawings decorative spandrels, similar to those used earlier on Scholes Hall on the University of New Mexico campus, are introduced. The square volutes on these spandrels, which were apparently to be of precast terra-cotta, contrast with running zigzags above the first-floor windows; the entry retains a Territorial flavor. The Simms Professional Building would have marked a further development in Meem's Pueblo Deco style, and it is a matter for regret that the

client, Mrs. Albert G. Simms, for various reasons did not build. John Gaw Meem records, Special Collections, Zimmerman Library, UNM. For further information on John Gaw Meem see Bainbridge Bunting, *John Gaw Meem: Southwestern Architect* (Albuquerque, University of New Mexico Press, 1983).

41. Maisel Building file, John Gaw Meem records, Special Collections, Zimmerman Library, University of New Mexico.

42. Ibid.

43. D. D. Dunne, *American Indian Painting of the Southwest and Plains* (Albuquerque: University of New Mexico Press, 1968).

44. The artists and their subjects are: Ha So De, *Navajo Ceremonial Hunt;* Theodore Suina, *Corn Maiden;* Olive Rush, *Pueblo Deer Dances, Navajo Mother and Child with Horse, Family in Cornfield;* Tony Martinez, *Thunderbirds;* Pablito Velarde, *Pueblo Women with Pottery;* Ben Quintana, *Bean Dancers;* Pop Chalee, *Wildlife;* Joe Herrera, *Butterfly Dancers;* Ignatius Palmer, *Apache Dancers;* A Twa Tsireh, *Corn Dance;* Harrison Begay, *Navajo Yei-bi-chei.*

45. Conversation between Carla Breeze and A. W. Boehning's son, Joe Boehning, who is also an architect, June 15, 1981.

46. According to Joe Boehning, his father had an extensive library of material related to the Southwest, particularly the Pueblos and Navajos.

47. The Wright Trading Post has since changed ownership and is now owned by American Business Interiors.

48. National Register of Historic Places Inventory: nomination form prepared by E. Threinen, 1978.

49. The thunderbird was another popular motif representing Indian culture to the designers who used it. Utilized by Pueblo potters, it appears in a more stylized form, and is related to fertility symbolism.

50. The Bassett Tower was first published in August 1930 in the *Western Architect* 39: 126; a photograph of the Luhrs Tower had been published in May 1930, in the *American Architect* 137: 58. Drawings for the Bassett Tower in the Ponsford/ Trost Collection, El Paso Public Library, are dated July 1929—that is, four months after bids for the Luhrs Tower were advertised for. (See note 28 above.)

51. For insights into the Islamic element in the ornament of the Kress Store we are indebted to Besim Hakim.

COLOR PLATES

PART THREE

Cochise County Courthouse,
Bisbee, Arizona, detail of parapet.

Cochise County Courthouse,
entrance.

Southern Pacific Station, Casa Grande, Arizona, band of precast stucco over windows and passenger entrance.

Arizona Biltmore Hotel, Phoenix, Arizona, cantilevered entrance.

Arizona Biltmore Hotel, roof line over entrance and lobby.

Arizona Biltmore Hotel, cast concrete block wall.

City-County Building, Phoenix, Arizona, general view.

City-County Building, flanking the west entrance.

City-County Building, cast concrete details at the roof line.

First Interstate Bank (Title and Trust) Building, Phoenix, Arizona, general view.

First Interstate Bank Building, light fixtures over the marquee on Adams Street entrance.

Kress Store, Phoenix, Arizona, facade above the first floor.

Luhrs Tower, Phoenix, Arizona, general view.

Luhrs Tower, entrance.

Valley National Bank Annex (Valley Bank Professional Building), Phoenix, Arizona, west entrance.

Valley National Bank Annex, decorative spandrels on the second and third stories.

Valley National Bank Annex, roof line details.

Winters Building, Phoenix, Arizona, general view from the northwest.

Reilly Funeral Home, Phoenix, Arizona, general view.

Albuquerque Indian Hospital, Albuquerque, New Mexico, east elevation.

Albuquerque Indian Hospital, stepped parapet on the first level.

KiMo Theater, Albuquerque, New Mexico, marquee after restoration.

KiMo Theater, detail of a terra-cotta shield.

Kimo Theater, terra-cotta corbel
on the east elevation.

Maisel Building, Albuquerque, New Mexico, recessed lobby.

Maisel Building, entrance with mural frieze.

Skinner Building, Albuquerque, New Mexico, general view.

Skinner Building, detail of parapet.

Wright's Trading Post, Albuquerque (now the Office Furniture Mart), facade of opalescent glass and aluminum.

Clovis Hotel, Clovis, New Mexico, general view.

Clovis Hotel, parapet.

100

Clovis Hotel, cantilever details.

Curry County Courthouse, Clovis, New Mexico, cast spandrels.

James M. Bickley School, Clovis, New Mexico, central entrance.

Shaffer Hotel, Mountainair, New Mexico, facade above the ground floor.

Roosevelt County Courthouse, Portales, New Mexico, cast concrete frieze above the entrance.

Colfax County Courthouse, Raton, New Mexico, zinc panels above the entrance.

Colfax County Courthouse, relief medallion.

Kress Store, Amarillo, Texas, general view.

Potter County Courthouse, Amarillo, Texas, general view.

Potter County Courthouse, terra-cotta panels.

White and Kirk Department Store, Amarillo, Texas, detail of terra-cotta panels.

Xerox Building, Amarillo, Texas, general view.

Bassett Tower, El Paso, Texas, general view.

Bassett Tower, setback with marble inlay.

Bassett Tower, terra-cotta details.

Bassett Tower, detail of entrance (transom grill).

Bassett Tower, cast terra-cotta details above the entrance.

Kress Store, El Paso, Texas, Mesa Avenue facade.

Kress Store, terra-cotta tiles and details on Mesa Avenue facade.

Kress Store, tower.

Kress Store, cast iron railing above the first-floor entrance on Mesa Avenue.

INDEX

Figures and plates are indexed by page number in *italic.*

121

INDEX

INDEX

INDEX